IMPROVING COMMUNICATION SKILLS

INTERACTIVE THEMATIC UNITS FOR PREVENTING CONFLICT

JOHN GUST, M.A.,
J. MEGHAN McCHESNEY
AND
RISA R. GECHTMAN

ILLUSTRATED BY ALEX GLIKIN

Teaching & Learning Company
1204 Buchanan St., P.O. Box 10
Carthage, IL 62321-0010

Cover photo by Images and More Photography

Copyright © 1997, Teaching & Learning Company

ISBN No. 1-57310-081-1

Printing No. 98765432

Teaching & Learning Company
1204 Buchanan St., P.O. Box 10
Carthage, IL 62321-0010

TLC10081 Copyright © Teaching & Learning Company, Carthage, IL 62321-0010

This book belongs to

_____

ACKNOWLEDGEMENTS

We would like to extend a heartfelt thanks to those individuals who have helped to make this book a reality:

From Meghan:
To Michael Arrigo, who has immensely improved my communication skills by both listening to and sharing thoughts, feelings and aspirations. I love you!

From John:
Thanks to Jill Eckhardt for all of her encouragement and support. "Just dandy!"

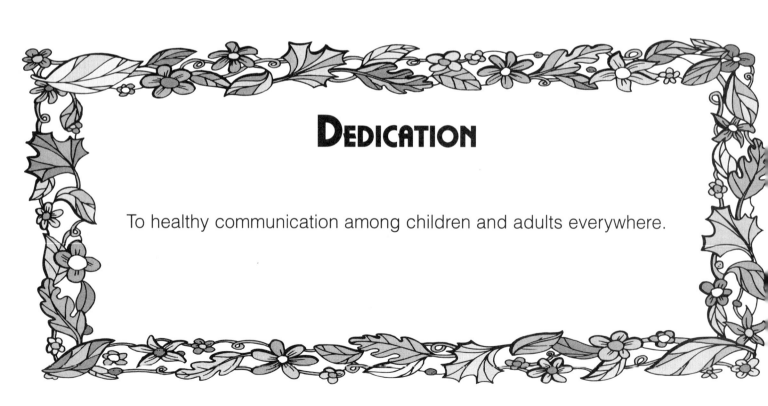

DEDICATION

To healthy communication among children and adults everywhere.

TABLE OF CONTENTS

INTERACTIVE THEMATIC UNITS

TALKING HONESTLY 7

LEARNING WITH OTHERS 36

SHARING FEELINGS 68

EXPLAINING WHAT YOU WANT 97

SPREADING PEACE 120

Dear Teacher or Parent,

Communication is a natural part of everyday life—we communicate all day long. Some people even say, "You cannot . . . not communicate!" It's unavoidable. Yet in spite of knowing how much and how important our communications are, it sometimes seems that we fail to pay attention to how well we communicate with others and how well others communicate with us. Typically, our communication patterns and habits, some good and some not so good, have been learned during our formative years from parents, guardians, other significant adults, siblings and peers.

This is a reason to start early. When we give our students the opportunity to notice and practice various communication skills, they will become more effective communicators and have more successful relationships. The more successful relationships a student has, the more pronounced the sense of belonging or connectiveness will be. And this, in turn, will raise their self-esteem.

The interactive thematic units and activities that we have provided in this book are designed to enhance your students' communication skills. The specific objectives of our activities are to help your students to:

- talk honestly with each other
- build listening and empathy skills
- discover their personal communication styles
- express their feelings appropriately
- develop good verbal and nonverbal communication skills
- practice assertiveness skills
- resolve conflicts
- increase the cooperativeness and learning in your classroom

Have fun!

Sincerely,

John, Meghan and Risa

TALKING HONESTLY

It appears then that genuine friendship cannot exist where one of the parties is unwilling to tell the truth and the other is equally indisposed to hear it.

–Cicero

What is most needed for our students to communicate effectively with others? Honesty. Simple to understand but not always easy to do. Speaking honestly requires a lot of work because when committing ourselves to talking honestly with one another, we set out on a rather difficult path. We *first* have to be honest with ourselves and *then* we have to be honest when communicating with others.

It takes plenty of courage to be honest with one another. Many times, in order to maintain somewhat shallow relationships, people focus on being polite and cordial, rather than being honest and straightforward. Politeness and courtesy are admirable qualities, but honesty from true friends is what is valued most of all.

Effective communicators are also consistent in words and action. We know that there are two basic causes for many misunderstandings. The first is not saying what we mean. The second is not doing what we say. When our students learn to say what they mean and do what they say, they become trustworthy communicators. The lack of alignment between word and action always results in a loss of power and effectiveness.

If our students are to become effective communicators, they must be motivated to ask themselves if it is more important to conform to what other people believe, or to discover what is true by acting on the desire and intent to see things as they really are. We must support a child's natural tendency to search for the truth.

Lastly, as teachers, we must show our students the virtue of talking honestly ourselves. When we do, our students will recognize the importance of keeping trust when they joyously exclaim, "You kept your promise!"

TALKING HONESTLY THEME OBJECTIVES

1. DEVELOP HONEST RELATIONSHIPS WITH YOUR STUDENTS

Be honest with your students. Let them know how you are feeling. When appropriate, share your feelings with your students. Tell the truth, openly and honestly. Listen to your students and really hear what they have to say. If your students are going to communicate effectively in your classroom, they must first trust you. The two most important components of a trusting relationship are honesty and openness. In a classroom where honesty is foremost, a student knows what to expect; there are no inconsistencies or surprises. Develop a trusting relationship with your students.

2. NURTURE CARING AND POSITIVE RELATIONSHIPS

Everybody wants to be cared for. But what does it mean to care? How does one act when truly caring for another? Do we help one another right into a state of dependency? Or do we really want to enable others to become all that they can–autonomous, responsible and respectful?

3. MODEL EFFECTIVE COMMUNICATION

It's been called modeling, observational learning, imitation, social learning and vicarious learning. If you want your students to develop good communication skills, you must show them the way. Ultimately, how you do that best is by living it. Be a good, honest, trusting and effective communicator!

4. SET REASONABLE CLASSROOM "AGREEMENTS"

Involve your students in the democratic process by defining which rules or "agreements" are to be kept by the class. By doing so you will help them to improve their negotiation and communication skills and also give them the message that you respect their thoughts and require them to be responsible for their actions. Jean Piaget wrote, "Rules imposed by external constraint remain external to the child's spirit. Rules due to mutual respect and cooperation take root inside the child's mind." Get your students communicating about what rules they want to live by in your classroom.

POSITIVELY POWERFUL

GOAL: Students will listen to their inhibiting thoughts and change them into positively powerful statements.

TIME: 20 minutes

SETTING: classroom

MATERIALS: "Positively Powerful" worksheet, pencil

PROCEDURE:

Your students have undoubtedly heard you say, "Now listen carefully!" a countless number of times. But how often have you asked students to listen to themselves? Your students can teach themselves about their self-concepts by listening to what they have to say–about themselves.

First, distribute the "Positively Powerful" worksheet. Ask your students to focus their attention to the top half of the sheet. Within a few minutes, your students should have a long list of examples under the "I have to . . ." side such as "come to school," "listen to my parents" and "do my homework" and an equally long list under the "I can't . . ." side such as "can't draw," "can't spell" and "can't do math."

Once your students have finished, instruct them to rewrite each of their negative "have to" and "can't" statements into "choose to" and "don't want to (badly enough)" statements. Several of your students may protest loudly! "Hey, teach"; retorts one, "I have to go to school; my mom makes me!" Challenge their thinking by asking, "Does your mom carry you to school each day?" "Does your mom physically force you to come?" As kids shake their heads "no," point out that they do choose to come to school each day. If they choose not to come, they would also be choosing to suffer the consequences! Likewise, a student may say, "But I can't get an A in spelling!" You can reply, "There's no way in the whole world that you could get an A?" The student may think for a minute and respond, "Well, maybe if I studied for hours every night and had someone help me and read a lot more." At which point you can say, "Ah-ha! So you can get an A if you want to badly enough!"

Give your students a few minutes to reread the second part of their worksheets with their positive and powerful new thoughts. Then discuss how their old self-concepts were negative. By saying "I have to" or "I can't," your students were inhibiting themselves and refusing to take responsibility for their actions. With a little listening and a slight change of mind, your students will learn to be honest enough to admit that they have power over their own thoughts and actions.

What kind of things do you believe you have to or can't do? Write your responses here.

I have to _____	**I can't** _____
I have to _____	**I can't** _____
I have to _____	**I can't** _____
I have to _____	**I can't** _____
I have to _____	**I can't** _____
I have to _____	**I can't** _____
I have to _____	**I can't** _____

Now rewrite each of your negative "have to" and "can't" statements into "choose to" and "don't want to (badly enough)" statements. Think about it. Are you really unable to, or do you really have to do the things you've mentioned?

I choose to _____	**I don't want to** _____
I choose to _____	**I don't want to** _____
I choose to _____	**I don't want to** _____
I choose to _____	**I don't want to** _____
I choose to _____	**I don't want to** _____
I choose to _____	**I don't want to** _____
I choose to _____	**I don't want to** _____

WE'RE TOTALLY A TEAM!

GOAL: Students will model effective team communications.

TIME: one hour

SETTING: classroom

MATERIALS: worksheets on pages 13-16, pencil

PROCEDURE:

Collaboration is the skill of the future. Research shows that students learn more effectively when working in cooperative teams. Similarly, businesses are increasingly organizing their employees in close-knit teams. To prepare our students for the future, we must teach them how to effectively communicate and problem-solve in a team setting.

This activity will test your students' problem-solving and communication abilities. Explain to your students that they will decide on a problem that they want to solve. It can be a problem in your room, school, community or the world. Second, each student will come up with individual solutions to the problem. Then the teammates will come together to brainstorm as a group. Finally, the team will choose a solution that they feel best addresses the issue. One of the team members will act as the Observer and therefore will not participate in the brainstorming.

To begin, help your class develop some brainstorming guidelines. Brainstorming is a group technique that involves the contribution of ideas by *all* members of the team. The objective is to create a list of ideas. It is not necessary to discuss each idea in detail (unless the meaning is unclear) and ideas are to be collected not accepted or rejected. Use these questions as prompts to develop some guidelines. We've provided a few possible answers. You may want to write the class' agreements on the board so the teams can refer to these guidelines as they brainstorm.

1. HOW COULD EACH TEAM MEMBER PREPARE FOR THE BRAINSTORMING SESSION?
Members should bring a few good ideas of their own to the session.

2. WHY IS IT IMPORTANT FOR EVERYONE TO CONTRIBUTE IDEAS TO THE TEAM?
Each person will have a different way of solving the problem. Ideas that seem silly at first may lead to a good solution.

3. DOES CRITICIZING A PERSON HELP OR HINDER THE TEAM? WHY?
Everyone needs to be encouraged at first. Later the ideas can be critiqued, but not the people.

4. IF YOU HEAR A GOOD IDEA, WHAT SHOULD YOUR TEAM DO?
Praise the person and build on the idea.

5. HOW DO YOU FEEL WHEN PEOPLE INTERRUPT YOU?
No one likes to be cut off, so no interruptions!

6. WHEN SHOULD YOU CRITIQUE AND ELIMINATE IDEAS?
Wait until all ideas have been presented, then discuss which ideas should be further explored.

Now that your students have established some brainstorming guidelines, determine what problem you'd like to tackle. Problems can be gleaned from the everyday interactions in your classroom, school or community. You can use this opportunity to facilitate and model effective brainstorming. Once your class has agreed on a problem, divide your class into groups of four to five students each. One person on the team will act as the Observer. Her job is to watch how the team functions by answering the questions on the "We're We Totally a Team?" worksheets on pages 14 and 15. The Observer should sit slightly away from her group. She may not participate in the brainstorming.

To begin, give each student a "We're Totally a Team!" worksheet on page 13. Have your students record the problem at the top of the worksheet. Allow each student to individually write several solutions to the problem. This should take about five minutes.

Next, have your students start brainstorming as a team. This is when the Observer starts answering the questions on her worksheets. Allow the teams 10 to 20 minutes to brainstorm. Remind the teams that you will be asking them for the team's best solution at the end of the activity. Once time is called, have a class discussion about each team's best solution.

Finally, the observers will share what they recorded on their worksheets. This should raise the class' awareness of the group roles and dynamics. To extend this activity, have your students complete the "We're Totally a Team Improvement Plan" worksheet on page 16.

Name _____

WE'RE TOTALLY A TEAM!

State the problem on the lines below.

_____

_____

Take a few minutes to write solutions to the problem by yourself.

1. _____

2. _____

3. _____

Now your team is ready to brainstorm. Write your team's solutions below. Remember the brainstorming guidelines! Your teacher will ask for the team's best solution at the end of the activity, so put your brains together!

1. _____

2. _____

3. _____

4. _____

5. _____

6. _____

7. _____

8. _____

9. _____

10. _____

OFFICIAL OBSERVER:

WERE WE TOTALLY A TEAM?

Your job is to be the Official Observer for your team. You must carefully watch how your group communicates and record your observations below. You cannot help your team brainstorm. As the Official Observer, it's important to be objective. That means no favorites and no put-downs!

1. Describe how each person helped the team.

Person 1: _____

_____

Person 2: _____

_____

Person 3: _____

_____

Person 4: _____

_____

2. Did someone become the team's leader? If yes, how?

_____

_____

3. Did everyone contribute equally? If no, why not?

_____

_____

4. Did some act as the encouragers for the team? Write what you heard them say.

_____

_____

Name _____

OFFICIAL OBSERVER:

WERE WE TOTALLY A TEAM?

5. Did some act as criticizers on the team? Write what you heard them say.

_____

_____

6. Did anyone talk about the best way to do this activity? What was the suggestion?

_____

_____

7. Did the team complete the "We're Totally a Team!" worksheet as a group or individually? How was this decided?

_____

_____

8. Did everyone contribute to the group? How did this happen?

_____

_____

9. How did the group resolve disagreements?

_____

_____

10. How did the group determine the best solution?

_____

_____

WE'RE TOTALLY A TEAM!
IMPROVEMENT PLAN

After listening to your team's Official Observer, complete this worksheet to improve your team's communication skills. By listening to other groups' Official Observers, you may learn some other ways of communicating effectively. You can use what you have learned the next time you are on a team.

Our team communicated best when we . . .

_____

_____

_____

_____

Our team did not communicate well when we . . .

_____

_____

_____

_____

Our team can improve by . . .

_____

_____

_____

_____

"Share"amony

GOAL: Students will experience giving and receiving.

TIME: one 60-minute and one 30-minute session conducted on consecutive days

SETTING: classroom

MATERIALS: *The Giving Tree* book, craft dough materials (see recipe on page 18), party music and decorations

PROCEDURE:

The steps to this activity are as follows:

• Read and discuss Shel Silverstein's book *The Giving Tree*.

• Have the students create an original craft dough gift to present to another student.

• Hold a giving ceremony in your classroom. Conduct this activity on two consecutive days–you will need a 60-minute block the first day and a 30-minute block on the second. All along the way, the "Share"amony activity celebrates the experience of giving.

Shel Silverstein's book contains a beautiful, ageless message about the gifts one gets and receives from giving. Giving is a gift that many people, including your students, may not often experience. Perhaps they feel they don't have enough for themselves. The touching irony with giving is, doing it usually triggers a series of positive experiences. When we give, it can be even more rewarding than receiving.

DAY 1

Read *The Giving Tree* to your class. Afterwards, compile a chart with your students to leave up as they begin to make their craft dough presents for one another.

What the Tree **Gave** to the Boy	What the Tree **Got** from the Boy

What the Boy **Gave** to the Tree	What the Boy **Got** from the Tree

Next, use the craft dough recipe below. The recipe makes enough dough for 10 students. Multiply the measurements according to your class size. You can make bowls of different color craft dough, as well, by adding food coloring. Pass out a fist-sized ball or equal amounts of different colored dough to each student.

Instruct students to create something with the dough–something that they would like to receive. They will create something for the express purpose of giving it away. Allow 30 minutes of quiet, creative time while your students make gifts. Then put the gifts someplace to dry where students can't see them. Affix a name tag to each gift so that you will be able to return the gifts discretely to the givers the following day.

DAY 2

Pass out pieces of newspaper along with the craft dough gifts and ask your students to wrap their presents. Next, let students pick a classmate's name out of a hat so that the receiver is randomly selected. The conclusion of your "Share"amony is near . . .

To make the event especially festive, decorate your room and play some party music–this will create an air of specialness. Now ask students to give their gifts to others. This part of the "Share"amony should celebrate both giving and receiving. After each student has both received and given a gift, ask students to reflect on what they liked more–giving or receiving. Also, ask students if they felt that giving had elements of getting in it.

This activity can be done many times throughout the school year. Simply alter the art materials to make it interesting for students. Providing multiple experiences of giving and receiving for students will help them to see as well as feel the gifts inherent in giving.

Craft Dough

3 cups (750 ml) flour

½ cup (125 ml) salad oil

½ cup (125 ml) water

food coloring

1. Add food coloring to the water until a desired shade is achieved.

2. Have students use their hands to mix flour, oil and colored water to turn the mixture into a ball.

3. Knead the ball well until it's ready to use.

4. Store the dough in an airtight container.

TALKING HONESTLY

18

COMMUNICATION CIRCLE

GOAL: Students will participate in a communications game and follow directions.

TIME: 30 minutes

SETTING: classroom

PROCEDURE:

Here is a creative way to get your students communicating. First, divide your class in half. Have students form two concentric circles. One half of your class will form the inner circle. The outer circle will face inward, while the inner circle faces outward. Each student should be facing a partner.

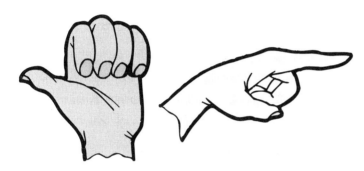  

Once students have formed their Communication Circle, you can explain the Communication Circle Hand Signals. Tell your class that when you hold your hands wide apart over your head, you are referring only to the outer circle. When you hold your hands close together over your head, you are referring only to the inner circle. The next signal you give will tell how many people they should pass when they move. When you hold up two fingers, then their circle should should pass two students in the other circle. The third signal tells students what direction to move. (When you point your thumb to the left, obviously they should walk to the left.) Bring your thumb and fingers together to signal the students to start talking. The final signal is the silent signal. When you clap your hands three times, they must stop talking.

Rehearse the signals. Hold your hands wide apart above your head, then hold up two fingers and point your thumb to the left. The students in the outer circle only should move left past two people in the inner circle. How did your students do?

Let's start communicating! You, or your students, can come up with a topic. Perhaps your students want to share their favorite subject at school or what they did over the weekend. (You can also use the Communication Circle to have students quiz each other on a lesson.) To begin, use your hand signal to indicate which circle will talk first. After a few minutes, clap three times and use your hand signal to indicate that it's the opposite circle's turn to talk. After another few minutes, clap three times and give the hand signal directions to instruct your class on how to change partners. Repeat this sequence until the majority of your class has communicated with each other. Your class should be impressed with themselves–not only are they communicating with each other verbally, they're communicating with you silently!

CREATING A COMMUNITY

GOAL: Students will share their thoughts and feelings with the class.

TIME: 30 minutes

SETTING: classroom

MATERIAL: an object such as a rock, feather or doll

PROCEDURE:

This activity provides a structure for your students to share their thoughts and feelings. To begin, have your students form a large circle either sitting on the floor or by rearranging their chairs. Next, explain the Creating a Community rules. They're short and simple. Number 1: You cannot talk unless you have the object in your hand. Number 2: If you do not want to answer the question, you have the right to pass.

Introduce the topic for the day and model an answer. Sentence starters work well. You may want to write the sentence starter on the board or on a sentence strip so students can refer to it as they formulate their responses. Once you have shared your response with the class, pass the object to the next speaker. You and your class will enjoy learning about each other's thoughts and feelings.

Here are some ideas to get started:

Lately I've been feeling . . .

I like _____ because . . .

Being a good friend means . . .

When I'm alone (happy, sad, hurt, angry), I like to . . .

When I'm alone, I feel . . .

If I could change anything, I would change . . .

I hate . . .

My favorite _____ is . . .

The last dream I remember was . . .

Last weekend . . .

I wish I knew more about . . .

I'm good at . . .

I'm most proud of . . .

I feel guilty (happy, sad, angry) when . . .

It's fun to . . .

If I were a _____, I would be . . .

My biggest fear is . . .

GET OUT OF MY SPACE!

GOAL: Students will become aware of comfortable and desirable body space when communicating with others.

TIME: 30 minutes

SETTING: classroom

PROCEDURE:

Every person has personal boundaries. Some people are open and sharing the first minute you meet them. Other people are more reserved and take time to get to know. People also have personal boundaries in terms of their body space. Some people like to be touched the first time you meet them, while other people may never feel comfortable being touched. This activity will help your students monitor their use of space.

Introduce the idea of body space to your students. The appropriate amount of space between a speaker and the listener depends on the situation. If you are telling someone a secret, most likely you will want to be physically close to them. You probably wouldn't want to shout your secret across the room! On the other hand, if you want to ask your friend on the other side of the playground about playing kickball, then yelling across the field may be the best way to communicate.

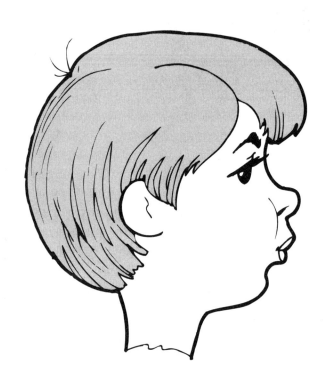
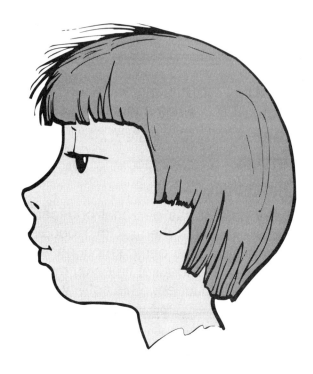

For this activity, your students are going to communicate semipersonal information to their partner over varying distances. First, have your class brainstorm a topic that they would like to discuss with a partner. For example, the partners may want to tell each other about their best birthday party or the worst thing that has ever happened to them. If you need some ideas, you may want to look at the sentence starters for the "Creating a Community" activity on page 20.

Now divide your class into pairs. Begin by having the partners stand facing each other with their noses about 3" (8 cm) apart (practically touching). Have one of the partners tell their story. After several minutes, ask your students to share how they feel talking to someone so close. Most of your students probably did not feel very comfortable!

Next have students stand about one foot apart. The second partner now tells his or her story. Discuss how they felt talking to their partner this time. Repeat this activity with partners standing arm's length away and then across the classroom. After each round of storytelling, discuss how the students' use of space affected the conversation. To conclude this activity, ask students to summarize what they learned about using space in effective communication. Hopefully they'll become more aware of their bodies and no one will have to tell them to "Get out of my space!"

I've Got My Eye on You!

> **GOAL:** Students will demonstrate direct eye contact while listening effectively to a partner.
>
> **TIME:** 30 minutes
>
> **SETTING:** classroom
>
> **PROCEDURE:**
>
> Good eye contact is another cornerstone to effective communication. Good eye contact usually means direct eye contact. The listener should look into the speaker's eyes without staring. A truly effective listener can monitor the speaker's amount of eye contact and reciprocate the same quantity. For "beginning" communicators, such as your students, focus on maintaining direct eye contact.

This activity will demonstrate to students how eye contact can affect conversations. Just as you did in the "Get Out of My Space!" activity, your class should brainstorm some discussion topics. Again, if you need some ideas, you may want to look at the sentence starters for the "Creating a Community" activity on page 20. Make sure your class chooses a topic that they can discuss for several minutes. Once the topic has been picked, have your students pair off. This time have students sit close together with their knees almost touching.

Your students are going to discuss the selected topic using six different kinds of eye contact. After each round of storytelling, ask students to discuss how they felt about their listening partner's level of eye contact. Give students several minutes to discuss the topic with 1) avoiding eye contact, 2) direct eye contact, 3) raising their eyebrows often, 4) staring, 5) winking and 6) occasionally glancing.

When students have completed this activity, they should know exactly how to keep their eyes on you, not to mention anyone else they talk to!

How Do I Sound?

GOAL: Students will learn how intonations effect their communications.

TIME: 30 minutes

SETTING: classroom

MATERIALS: worksheets on pages 25 and 26

PROCEDURE:

Voice intonation is yet another foundation of effective communication. If you want to communicate that you find someone amusing, you may want to comment with a laugh. If you are angry with a person, raising your voice will help communicate your message.

To begin the lesson, reproduce and cut up enough of the "How Do I Sound? Kinds of Voices" worksheet and the "How Do I Sound? Phrases" worksheet so that each student in your class receives one description of a voice and one phrase.

To begin the lesson, ask your students to brainstorm different kinds of voices. Then hand out one piece of the "Kinds of Voices" worksheet and one strip of the "Phrases" worksheet to each student. Some phrases will be repeated. Each student in your class is going to read a phrase using the kind of intonation described on the "Kinds of Voices" paper. Each student reads the phrase with the appropriate voice, then asks the class, "How do I sound?" The class then describes what the student's intonation communicated. You may want the students who have the same phrase but different voices, or intonations, to read the phrases in succession so that your class can compare the differences in message. You may also want to trade phrases to test the different voices. Your students may be surprised how much difference a change in intonation can have on the message!

Finally, conclude this lesson with a discussion about how different intonations can aid the message that you wish to send to the listener. For additional practice, have students read a story and use the correct intonations to communicate the character's moods.

HOW DO I SOUND?
KINDS OF VOICES

Cut this worksheet along the dashed lines. Each student in your class will need one piece.

groaning	hesitant	laughing
signing	tired	mumbling
happy	shouting	whispering
whine-y	questioning	bored
crying	begging	sarcastic
amusing	angry	tattletale
serious	timid	scared

How Do I Sound?
PHRASES

Cut this worksheet along the dashed lines. Each student in your class will need one strip.

Put that paper away.	Go to your room.
Push in your chair.	How much does it cost?
Clean up the mess.	Where are my glasses?
I hate you!	Take out the garbage.
I love you!	Please pass the ketchup.
Go away!	Come here.
Why did you do that?	Next, please.
What's going on?	Who's there?
Can you help me?	Hello!
What time is it?	May I go to the bathroom?

26

STUDENTS RULE!

GOAL: Students will set reasonable class rules or "agreements."

TIME: 30 minutes

SETTING: classroom

MATERIALS: worksheet on page 28

PROCEDURE:

Traditionally, teachers have set down the law of the land or the law of the classroom, as the case may be, and students dutifully followed. Today, schools are changing. More and more kids are asking to be taken seriously, they want to feel that what they say and feel amounts to something. It may be time in your classroom to come up with a new set of guidelines of rules! As we currently strive to help our students be more responsible for themselves, we should be sure to include them in setting class agreements.

You may be surprised at how strict your students are with themselves. And your students are more likely to follow "rules" that they helped to develop. Suddenly you'll find you and your students are "agreeing" on how to behave, instead of you trying to "rule" their behavior!

Name _____

STUDENTS RULE!

Students rule? What does that mean? It means that it's all up to you! You get to decide. Decide on what? You get to decide on exactly what rules your classroom should have.

Now you have all this added responsibility. You're in school to learn and now you have to decide upon all the ways you and your classmates will behave in order to make learning most effective.

First, think of at least five value words that will describe how you want your classroom to be. Here's a few examples: Do you want your classroom to be clean, messy, quiet, noisy, nurturing, mean, friendly or disrespectful? Write five value words below.

Next, decide exactly how you want people to behave in order to uphold those value words you chose. Make sure you write your rules in the form of a behavior that you will be able to see other students doing.

_____   _____   _____

_____   _____

1. _____

2. _____

3. _____

4. _____

5. _____

When you have finished writing your ideas for classroom rules, get together with a group of about four to six of your classmates and decide together which rules you'd like for your classroom. When you're done, you can share your rules with the whole class. Then the whole class can decide which rules to live by in your classroom.

Is Your Lie Detector Working?

> **GOAL:** Students will learn to identify their response to dishonesty.
>
> **TIME:** 30 minutes
>
> **SETTING:** classroom
>
> **MATERIALS:** "Is Your Lie Detector Working?" worksheet, pencils
>
> **PROCEDURE:**
>
> When we tell a lie, our bodies usually have a reaction. Somewhere inside, we feel off kilter. Honesty also provokes a bodily response–one of ease. The purpose of this activity is to let students experience their internal "lie detectors" or their body's reaction to telling lies.

It is interesting to note that our internal "lie detectors" help law enforcement personnel determine if people are telling the truth. Lie detector machines measure and record the body's physiological response to questions. Experts review the data and are often able to determine if the subject replied truthfully.

To begin this activity, say to your students, "Right now we are going to get really quiet in order to listen to our bodies. Then we will work with a partner to experience how our bodies react when we lie. If you pay close attention to your body, you may notice a tight feeling, as if you are tied up in knots. When you are honest, you don't experience this crunched up feeling." This information may spark a discussion. Allow time for this, if necessary.

66 Now, let's close our eyes and take a deep breath. Hold it for a few seconds (count one, two, three). Let it out." Repeat this procedure a few times. Ask participants if they can identify any body sensations. Do they feel relaxed? That is the state that you want them to experience.

As soon as the majority of your students have quieted themselves and have begun to listen to their bodies, hand out the worksheet on page 31 to everyone. Each question on the sheet asks the students to respond honestly and then also dishonestly to a statement. Give your students about 15 minutes to complete the worksheet.

After they finish, take a few more deep breaths with your students, instructing them again to listen in to the sounds and sensations of their bodies. Now, pair each student with a partner. Instruct students to take turns asking each other questions, one at a time.

RULES

1. When the Questioner asks the question, the Answerer can choose to either answer with the truth or with a lie.
2. After a question is posed and an answer is given, the Questioner is to guess if a lie was told.
3. The Answerer must now be truthful regardless of his or her previous answer.
4. The Answerer comments on bodily reactions to his or her answer (for example, "I felt weird telling the lie.").
5. Answerers should lie at least once to experience how their bodies react.

As a debriefing say, "Telling one lie often requires telling another lie, and the truth gets farther and farther away from us. The more lies you tell, the less sensitive your internal lie detector is. It's very sad when this mechanism in us stops working."

Name _____

IS YOUR LIE DETECTOR WORKING?

Answer each question on this sheet with the TRUTH and then a LIE. For example, for the first question you will write your name next to the T for TRUTH. Then write a made-up name for yourself on the line next to the L for LIE. Answer the rest of the questions the same way. You will go over your answers with a partner after you complete this sheet.

1. What is your name?

T: _____

L: _____

2. Where are you from?

T: _____

L: _____

3. What's your favorite subject in school?

T: _____

L: _____

4. How do you feel right now?

T: _____

L: _____

5. If you could change something about yourself, what would it be?

T: _____

L: _____

6. Which do you like better, chocolate or vanilla ice cream?

T: _____

L: _____

7. Can you speak more than one language? If yes, which one?

T: _____

L: _____

EACH TIME YOU LIE TO YOUR PARTNER, ANSWER THE QUESTION "HOW DID IT FEEL TO LIE?"

Use these lines to write your responses.

1. _____

_____

2. _____

_____

3. _____

_____

4. _____

_____

5. _____

_____

6. _____

_____

7. _____

_____

CONSTRUCTING COMMUNICATION

GOAL: Students will practice constructive communication through a series of role plays.

TIME: 40 minutes

SETTING: classroom

MATERIALS: "Constructing Communication" worksheets

PROCEDURE:

Very often children communicate in blunt, alienating ways. It is important to teach them how to ask for what they want and need as well as to assert themselves when being mistreated. Instead of relying on you, the teacher, to solve their daily disputes, this activity will give students the language and experience to handle situations constructively.

First, generate a list of words on the chalkboard that have to do with constructive communication. You can ask the question, "What qualities make a good communicator?" Start the list with these words and phrases: *honesty, directness, firm but polite, eye contact, a strong voice, good listening skills.* Add and discuss students' answers to the question.

Then let your students know that you would like them to try to incorporate the qualities listed as they respond to different scenarios. They will first respond individually, on the "Constructing Communication" worksheet. After the worksheets have been completed, let different students role-play the scenarios until you are satisfied that they understand how to alter their language and style towards a constructive communication mode.

A final word: Using constructive communication is like building a bridge to another person, rather than creating a roadblock.

TALKING HONESTLY

CONSTRUCTING COMMUNICATION

1. You are in the school auditorium. The person seated behind you has their feet on the back of your chair. How can you let the person know you are bothered? _____

   _____

   _____

2. Someone has cut in front of you in line. You usually ignore it when this happens. Today you want to speak up for yourself. What will you say? _____

   _____

   _____

3. You have been raising your hand for what feels like a half hour. Your teacher continues to ignore you in order to quiet students who are fighting or calling out. How can you let her know that you would like some attention, too? _____

   _____

   _____

4. You struck out in a game of softball, and one of your teammates calls you a failure. Since you don't intend to give up the game, how do you tell your teammate that you did your best and don't like to be called names? _____

   _____

   _____

5. You are working with a group of students. Every time you open your mouth to speak, others interrupt you. How do you tell your group that you would like them to listen to you?

   _____

   _____

Literature in Support of Talking Honestly

The Adventures Through the Black Hole by Jeong-Soon Kim (Hollym), 1993

A Big Fat Enormous Lie by Marjorie W. Sharmat (Dutton), 1986

A Calf for Christmas by Astrid Lindgren (Farrar, Straus & Giroux), 1991

The Cat That Could Spell Mississippi by Laura Hawkins (Houghton), 1992

Coaching Ms. Parker by Carla Heymsfeld (Bradbury), 1992

The Cold & Hot Winter by Johanna Hurwitz (Morrow), 1988

The Emperor's New Clothes by Hans Christian Andersen (Dutton), 1991

Eppie M. Says by Olivier Dunrea (Macmillan), 1990

Ever After by Rachel Vail (Orchard), 1994

The Fantastic Stay-Home-from-School Day by N. Hayashi (Dutton), 1992

Five Finger Discount by Barthe DeClements (Delacorte), 1989

Fox Tale by Yossie Abolafia (Greenwillow), 1991

Freya's Fantastic Surprise by Libby Hathorn (Scholastic/Hardcover), 1989

The Giving Tree by Shel Silverstein (Harper), 1994

Hanna's Hog by Jim Aylesworth (Atheneum), 1988

Ira Sleeps Over by Bernard Waber (Houghton), 1973

I Want Answers and a Parachute by P.J. Peterson, (Simon & Schuster), 1993

Jace the Ace by Joanne Rocklin (Macmillan), 1990

Josie's Beau by Natalie Honeycutt (Avon), 1988

The King Has Horse's Ears by Peggy Thomson (Simon & Schuster), 1988

Liars by P.J. Peterson (Simon & Schuster), 1991

The Magic Fort by Juanita Havill (Houghton), 1991

Mean Streak by Ilene Cooper (Morrow), 1991

Ottie Slockett by Ida Luttrell (Dial), 1990

The Pickle Song by Barthe DeClements (Viking), 1993

Pinocchio by Carlo Collodi, adapted by Catherine D. Weir (Random), 1996

The Principal's New Clothes by Stephanie Calmenson (Scholastic), 1991

A Question of Trust by Marion Bauer (Scholastic/Hardcover), 1994

Rabbit Rambles On by Susanna Gretz (Four Winds), 1992

Rhoda, Straight and True by Roni Schotter (Lothrop), 1986

The Shiniest Rock of All by Nancy Patterson (Farrar), 1991

The Signmaker's Assistant by Tedd Arnold (Dial), 1992

Sixth Grade Secrets by Louis Sachar (Scholastic), 1992

Sub by P.J. Peterson (Dutton), 1993

The Surprise Party by Annabelle Prager (Random), 1988

The Winged Cat by Deborah Lattimore (HarperCollins), 1992

Your Move, J.P.! by Lois Lowry (Houghton), 1990

LEARNING WITH OTHERS

INTERDEPENDENCE

*It is the province of knowledge to speak,
and it is the privilege of wisdom to listen.*

–Oliver Wendell Holmes, Jr.

If your students are going to learn with each other, they will need to first of all care about those others. The root of caring is something we call *rapport*. Rapport stems from emotional attunement and the capacity for empathy. The ability to sense how someone else feels is needed in a wide variety of situations, from learning together, working and social action, to teaching and playing. The lack of empathy is also revealing; the trait is deficient in criminal sociopaths, rapists and child molesters.

Have you ever noticed how people's emotions are rarely put into words? More often they are expressed through other means. Therefore, the silent secret to intuiting another's feelings is in the ability to read nonverbal cues: tone of voice, gesture, facial expressions and the like. When words disagree with one of these channels, the emotional truth is in *how* something is said rather than in *what* is said. One key point in communications research is that 90% or more of an emotional message is nonverbal. These messages–sensing anxiety in someone's tone of voice, irritation in the quickness of a gesture–are almost always taken in unconsciously, without paying attention to the nature of the verbal message.

The other key element needed in learning with others is the neglected communication skill of listening. Most people don't really know how to listen! The results of ineffective listening are typically: half-understood directions, erroneous actions and misdirected work. When students learn to really listen, they will become better able to deal with conflict, handle emotional situations, solve problems, confront effectively and follow directions. Imagine what all of that could do for learning with others!

When effectively learning with others, it becomes imperative that students learn the skills of empathetic understanding and adequate listening.

LEARNING WITH OTHERS THEME OBJECTIVES

1. DEVELOP EMPATHY SKILLS

Empathy is the human quality that leads us to override self-interest and act with compassion and altruism. If students are going to learn with each other in the current trend of cooperative groups, they will benefit from being able to get in touch with the way another is feeling. Teach your students to become more empathetic.

2. DEVELOP LISTENING SKILLS

We all know that communication as a skill is a rather common concept. But the thought of listening as a skill is somewhat unfamiliar. But did you know that of all the time we spend communicating, by far the greatest amount of time is spent listening? Listening as a modality of absorbing information is used far more than reading and writing combined. It is the method used most often for learning. Unfortunately, however, listening is the least understood modality of all! Listening takes more than just the simple mental process of hearing. True listening requires energy and discipline. Help your students to develop the discipline to become effective listeners.

3. BECOME SKILLED IN READING THE FORM OF NONVERBAL COMMUNICATION CALLED BODY LANGUAGE

We all communicate without using words. As we speak we project messages not only with our words but also with our bodies. The way we sit, stand, walk, offer facial expressions and move our bodies are indicators to our thoughts and feelings. The way we dress also provides evidence of our attitudes and beliefs. When students become aware of the fact that it is nearly impossible to provide a verbal message without also speaking with the body, they become more effective communicators. They learn to "read" the nonverbal cues which offer additional information that can help to elucidate any verbal message.

WHAT ABOUT LEARNING TO LISTEN?

> **GOAL:** Students will become aware of how much of their day is spent listening and determine the need to improve listening skills.
>
> **TIME:** 25 minutes
>
> **SETTING:** classroom
>
> **MATERIALS:** worksheet on page 39, pencil
>
> **PROCEDURE:**
>
> In most schools in the United States (and around the world for that matter), teachers emphasize the three Rs–reading, 'riting and 'rithmetic. Recently, we have become very creative about how we teach these subjects in relation to the rest of the curriculum, but we still tend to stress language arts and mathematics. But are we teaching what are students need to be productive workers?

Surprisingly, when researchers studied what skills people use in the work force, they found that we teachers are neglecting to teach the most often used skill! When studying communication time in schools and at work, these researchers discovered that 50 to 60% of each person's day is spent listening. And when you consider how little time we actually spend teaching children listening skills (as opposed to reading, writing or speaking skills), you can imagine that our schools are not producing the most prepared workers-to-be.

Fortunately though, you can teach your students good listening skills! The first step in cultivating good listeners is to make students aware of how important and relevant listening is to their future. So let's get started! First, distribute the "What About Learning to Listen?" worksheet to students. Have them estimate the amount of time they spend reading, writing, speaking and listening in a typical day at school in percentages. Then have your students estimate how much time an adult they know spends doing these same activities at work. Below your students' percentages, they can draw a bar graph that depicts their estimations. You might surprise your students with the real numbers:

At School		At Work	
Reading	15-20%	Reading	10-20%
Writing	10-15%	Writing	5-15%
Speaking	10-20%	Speaking	20-30%
Listening	**50-60%**	Listening	**50-60%**

Now have students draw the true percentages on the Actual Students' Communication Time and Actual Employees' Communication Time graphs on page 39. Finally, have your students compare and contrast their estimations with the actual percentages. This activity should convince students of the importance of listening!

Name _____

WHAT ABOUT LEARNING TO LISTEN?

Is listening an important and useful skill? You bet it is! And you are going to prove it. First, let's see how often you think you read, write, speak and listen at school in terms of percentages. What about an adult at work? Record your estimations on the lines below.

STUDENTS AT SCHOOL
Reading _____%
Writing _____%
Speaking _____%
Listening + _____%
100%

EMPLOYEES AT WORK
Reading _____%
Writing _____%
Speaking _____%
Listening + _____%
100%

Then make a bar graph to illustrate your estimations.

Estimated Students' Communication Time

	Reading	Writing	Speaking	Listening
100%				
90%				
80%				
70%				
60%				
50%				
40%				
30%				
20%				
10%				
0%				

Estimated Employees' Communication Time

	Reading	Writing	Speaking	Listening
100%				
90%				
80%				
70%				
60%				
50%				
40%				
30%				
20%				
10%				
0%				

Now listen to your teacher read the actual communication times. Make a bar graph with this information. Compare the four graphs.

Actual Students' Communication Time

	Reading	Writing	Speaking	Listening
100%				
90%				
80%				
70%				
60%				
50%				
40%				
30%				
20%				
10%				
0%				

Actual Employees' Communication Time

	Reading	Writing	Speaking	Listening
100%				
90%				
80%				
70%				
60%				
50%				
40%				
30%				
20%				
10%				
0%				

SHHH! LISTEN!

GOAL: Students will listen to their surroundings.

TIME: five minutes

SETTING: classroom

MATERIAL: "Shhh! Listen!" worksheet for each student

PROCEDURE:

This activity is not only good for increasing your students' ability to listen, it is also a great way to calm them down after recess!

As your students come back in the room, ask them to sit down quietly, put their feet flat on the floor and place their hands flat on their desks. All at once say, "Shhh! Listen! What was that?" as you cock your head to the side slightly. If a student moves or makes a noise, say, "And that?" Then invite your students to keep listening intently for several minutes. Then, without saying a word, pass out the "Shhh! Listen!" worksheet. Then as quietly as possible, pick up a piece of chalk and write, *Read the directions on the worksheet and do as it asks*, on the chalkboard. After they have had several minutes to write their responses, they should, as the worksheet explains, pass their worksheet to a partner without talking. Once the partners have had a chance to view the other's worksheets, verbally ask them to share all that they heard.

You may want to repeat this activity for several days and watch as your students learn to name many specific sounds. If you have problems with students giggling or making noises, before you start this activity tell your students that you're going to watch to see who's intelligent enough to listen quietly. You're even willing to bet that several students won't be able to sit still and listen. Watch them make every effort to prove you wrong. Your students will be challenged to listen more carefully, and you can tell them how pleased you are with their awesome intelligence and listening abilities!

Make sure you point out to your students that we hear all kinds of sounds every day but rarely listen to them. You may also want to point out to your class that they just did a fabulous job of listening. But now that you know they can listen, anytime you catch them not listening in the future, it is because they choose not to . . . and that's breaking the rules!

Name _____

Shhh! Listen!

Now that you have spent the last few minutes listening, let's see if you can remember, and list, all of the different things that you heard. What's that? You say you didn't hear anything? What about your own breathing? The clock? The shuffling of someone's feet on the ground? How about that bird singing outside? What about the wind? Maybe you could even hear the sizzling of the sun? Who knows! What did you hear?

1. _____

2. _____

3. _____

4. _____

5. _____

6. _____

7. _____

8. _____

9. _____

10. _____

11. _____

12. _____

Now, without talking, trade and compare your list with a partner. Did they hear something that you weren't aware of? Imagine that! How does it feel to just sit totally still without having to do anything except listen? Is it relaxing?

When your teacher signals, share your findings with the rest of the class.

HOW WELL DO I LISTEN?

GOAL: Students will evaluate how effectively they listen.

TIME: 30 minutes

SETTING: classroom

MATERIALS: "How Well Do I Listen?" worksheet for each student, pencil

PROCEDURE:

To become more effective listeners, students need to assess their strengths and weaknesses. If they are aware of their weaknesses when it comes to listening, they'll be able to focus on improving in these areas. Listening involves many different skills. Have students read each question and check the box that applies to them.

Once your students have finished the checklist, help them rate themselves.

If your students have the highest scores in "Almost Always" and "Often," then they actively listen. This means that they generally acknowledge and respond to the speaker, concentrate on the main ideas, avoid being distracted and pay attention to the message the speaker is conveying–not just the words. These students are truly listening.

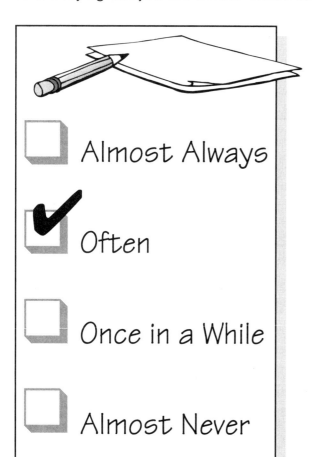

If your students score highest in "Often" and "Once in a While," then they hear but do not truly listen. This means that the student hears words and sounds, but they are not searching for meaning and understanding. Misunderstandings often occur since they are not concentrating on what is being said, even though they appear to be listening.

If your students score highest in "Once in a While" and "Almost Never," then they are half hearing. This means that they listen for a bit, then sign off. They mainly pay attention to themselves, not other speakers. Often, they only listen to figure out when they can have their turn to talk. These students would rather be heard, than hear.

Finally, encourage your students to set goals for themselves. Have them choose one or two areas where they feel they need improvement. They should pay special attention to the activities provided that work on each of these skills. And don't forget to have your students pat themselves on the back for the areas that they have mastered!

Name _____

HOW WELL DO I LISTEN?

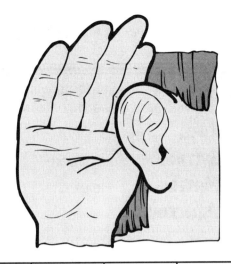

Read each question and put a check in the box that best describes yourself. When you finish, count the number of checks in each column. Then listen to your teacher to rate your listening ability.

		ALMOST ALWAYS	OFTEN	ONCE IN A WHILE	ALMOST NEVER
1.	Do I concentrate on all conversations, no matter what is being said?				
2.	Do I listen even if I think I know what is going to be said?				
3.	Do I repeat what the speaker has said to myself?				
4.	Do I look at the speaker?				
5.	Do I ask questions when I do not understand the speaker?				
6.	Do I avoid daydreaming?				
7.	Do I avoid forming an argument if I disagree with the speaker?				
8.	Do I listen for the main idea as well as facts?				
9.	Do I focus on the speaker's words and not how they look?				
10.	Do I take notes when I need to?				
11.	Do I hear sounds without being distracted?				
12.	Do I listen to the speaker without criticizing them?				
13.	Do I pay attention to directions the first time they are given?				
14.	Do I pay attention to the speaker's words, tone of voice and body language?				
15.	Do I spend time every day listening to myself?				

HELP!

GOAL: Students will listen to a story read to them and repeat what they have heard.

TIME: 20 minutes

SETTING: classroom

MATERIALS: "Help! Quiz" per student, pencil

PROCEDURE:

Here's another fun way to assess your students' listening skills. First, complete the "Help! Story" worksheet. You or one designated student should fill in the blanks to complete the story.

Once you've finished this task, tell your students that you are going to read a story with certain directions. You are only going to give the directions once, so they must listen carefully. No one can ask questions. At the end of the story they will be quizzed, so it's a good idea to take notes. Read the "Help! Story" slowly and carefully.

When you've finished reading the story, pass out the "Help! Quiz." Then check the answers as a class. The answers to the first part are 3, 5, 8, 7, 4, 1, 2, 6. The answers to the second part will vary depending on how you fill in the blanks.

Finally, your students should postulate why they did or did not do well on the quiz. What did they do when listening that helped them to remember the story? What was not helpful? How could they listen better in the future? Hopefully your students will be able to help the characters in the story and help themselves improve their listening skills, too!

Name _____

HELP! STORY

Fill in the blanks below before reading this story to the class.

Professor _____ (woman's name) was an eccentric woman. She lived in a small, cluttered house not far from _____ (name) University where she taught physics. When not teaching, she was at home working on a time travel machine. You are a student in her class. After noticing that she was absent for _____ (number) days, you decided to check on her.

Since she didn't answer your knock on her door, you opened the door and heard Professor _____ (professor's name) mumbling in the back room. You called out, "Professor, are you okay?" Startled, the professor jumped back and knocked over a mysterious _____ (adjective) box. Suddenly you saw a bright _____ (color) flash of light, and you felt yourself rising to the ceiling. "Oh no!" the Professor cried, "I've activated the time machine!" "Help!" you screamed as you looked down and saw your _____ (body part) disappearing. She quickly threw you a tape recorder and said, "If you want to return to the present, you must follow these directions. Good luck!" And you disappeared only to find yourself back in the year _____ (after the 1700s).

You shake your head in disbelief and look at the tape player. "Well," you think, "Pressing *play* may help me get out of this mess.'" This is what you heard:

If you ever wish to get back to the future, you must first find a person by the name of _____ (man's name). He is my _____ (relative). He lives in _____ (city). Knock on his door _____ (number) times. When he answers, say_____(silly phrase). Ask him for _____ (object) and _____ (object).

Take these two items to the town square at _____ (time) o'clock on the first _____ (day) of _____ (month). However, if the moon is full, wait _____ (number) more days and buy a bag of candy from the beggar. Now walk to the large fountain in the middle of the square. Ask the third boy you see to take the two items to the middle of the fountain and hold them high above his head. He will do this for some candy. Look to the sky for a crow. When it cries three times, turn to the boy and shout the secret word _____! (word). If you follow these directions precisely, you should arrive safely home by _____ (time) the next day.

Name _____

HELP! QUIZ

Now that you've heard all of your instructions, let's see how good a listener you are. Will you be able to help yourself get back to the future?

What order were the directions given to you? Number the instructions from one to eight.

____ Go to the town square

____ Walk to the fountain

____ Shout secret word

____ Look for the crow

____ Buy candy

____ Find the man

____ Get the two objects

____ Tell the boy to stand in the fountain

Now answer these questions:

1. What did the professor teach? _____

2. How many days was she absent? _____

3. What color light flashed from the box? _____

4. What year were you sent to? _____

5. What was the professor's relative's name? _____

6. What phrase were you supposed to say to her relative? _____

_____

7. What city did the relative live in? _____

8. What were you to do if the moon was full? _____

9. Where was the fountain? _____

10. What day did you arrive home? _____

TLC10081 Copyright © Teaching & Learning Company, Carthage, IL 62321-0010

CHECK, CHECK, CHECK FOR LISTENING

GOAL: Students will understand and practice the basic skills of good listening.

TIME: 25 minutes

SETTING: classroom

MATERIALS: "Check, Check, Check for Listening" worksheet for each student and one "Check, Check, Check for Listening Homework Sheet" for each student.

PROCEDURE:

Your students may need some practice listening. This activity is a great way for your students to check, check, check for listening while they learn more about each other.

First, explain to your students the "Check, Check, Check for Listening" worksheet. Explain that sometimes a friend needs someone to just listen to their problems, thoughts or feelings. They want an "ear," not a "mouth." They don't want to hear solutions, they just want to be heard. Once your students understand the characteristics of good listening, have them find a partner. Partners should sit facing each other in chairs with their knees almost touching. Partners should then decide who is Partner A and who is Partner B. You may want to model the following steps before your students begin.

Explain that Partner A is going to be given three speaking prompts to complete. He or she will have exactly one minute to complete each prompt while Partner B carefully listens. Partner B will then have to reflect back what Partner A said in a type of listening check for each speaking prompt. Partner B will use the listening check prompt or sentence stem to verify that they listened to what Partner A was saying.

Here are the three speaking and listening prompts. Have Partner A complete each speaking prompt and Partner B complete each listening prompt before changing roles.

Number 1

Speaking Prompt: Partner A: I usually dream about . . .

Listening Prompt: Partner B: What I hear you saying is . . .

Number 2

Speaking Prompt: Partner A: I hate it when . . .

Listening Prompt: Partner B: You feel . . .

Number 3

Speaking Prompt: Partner A: What I like best about school is . . .

Listening Prompt: Partner B: It sounds as if . . .

Once Partners A and B complete the three prompts, have Partner A complete the "Check, Check, Check for Listening" worksheet. They will be evaluating or rating their partner to determine how well they felt listened to. Once Partner A has completed the evaluative listening worksheet, have your students switch roles. Partner B will now answer the speaking prompts to check his or her understanding. Then have Partner B fill out the "Check, Check, Check for Listening" worksheet to evaluate Partner A's listening skills.

Finally, discuss with your class how they felt when their partner was listening to them. See who can list good listening habits (the do's).

EXTENSION

Have your students take home a "Check, Check, Check for Listening Homework Sheet" to practice listening to someone at home. Have them use the alternative set of speaking and listening prompts to use at home. Who knows, maybe a mom, dad, grandparent, brother or sister may appreciate an ear!

Have your students write these three speaking and listening prompts to complete at home with a partner:
Speaker: When I'm at home with you, I feel . . .
Listener: You feel . . .

Speaker: The best thing about my day was . . .

Listener: It sounds like . . .

Speaker: What I appreciate about you is . . .

Listener: What I hear you saying is . . .

Speaker: When I'm at home with you, I feel . . .

Listener: You feel . . .

Name _____

CHECK, CHECK, CHECK FOR LISTENING

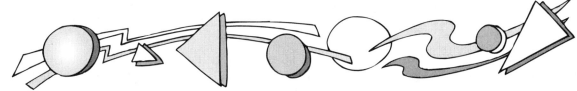

Sometimes you need someone who will just listen to your problems, thoughts or feelings. A good listener follows the easy rules listed. After you and your listener have followed the three speaking and listening prompts your teacher has provided, check those boxes that you feel your listener has followed well. Were they a good listener? Did you feel heard?

Speaker's name: _____

Listener's name: _____

DO . . .

❑ listen to understand
❑ look at the speaker's eyes
❑ relax!
❑ face the speaker
❑ nod your head at the right time
❑ lean forward slightly
❑ match your facial expression with their feelings

Number of boxes checked _____

DON'T . . .

❑ listen to judge or criticize
❑ interrupt
❑ ask questions
❑ give advice

Number of boxes checked _____

Total number of boxes checked _____

Name _____

CHECK, CHECK, CHECK FOR LISTENING
HOMEWORK SHEET

Sometimes you need someone who will just listen to your problems, thoughts or feelings. A good listener follows the easy rules listed. After you and your listener have followed the three speaking and listening prompts your teacher has provided, check those boxes that you feel your listener has followed well. Were they a good listener? Did you feel heard?

Speaker's name: _____

Listener's name: _____

DO . . .

❏ listen to understand
❏ look at the speaker's eyes
❏ relax!
❏ face the speaker
❏ nod your head at the right time
❏ lean forward slightly
❏ match your facial expression with their feelings

Number of boxes checked _____

DON'T . . .

❏ listen to judge or criticize
❏ interrupt
❏ ask questions
❏ give advice

Number of boxes checked _____

Total number of boxes checked _____

Speaker's name: _____

Relation to listener: _____

Was _____ a good listener? Why or why not? _____

_____

Did you feel heard? Why or why not? _____

_____

CHILDREN SHOULD BE HEARD

GOAL: Students will assess the effects of negative messages through a creative writing exercise.

TIME: 45 minutes

SETTING: classroom

MATERIALS: "Children Should Be Heard" worksheet for each student, pencils

PROCEDURE:

Children frequently hear comments like:

"Be quiet."
"Hush."
"Shut up."
"Don't speak unless you are spoken to."
"Children should be seen but not heard."
"Don't talk back to me!"
"Who do you think you are talking like that?"
"Don't interrupt me while I'm talking."
"Open up those ears."
"Look at me when I talk to you."
"Why can't you pay better attention?"
"Hello . . . wake up . . . pay attention."

The messages are usually used to encourage children to become better listeners. In reality, these messages cause negative feelings. Instead of serving as encouragement, they create an association between low self-esteem and listening. Positive, encouraging messages sound entirely different:

"If you can wait for a minute, I'd be happy to listen to what you have to say."

"I'd appreciate you hearing me out, then I'll listen to your thoughts and feelings."

"I like it when you listen to me."

"Thank you for listening."

"I value your opinions, even if I don't agree with them."

"Could you lower your voice?"

Most of your students are not aware of how the negative messages they hear affect their desire to listen. For this activity, pass out the accompanying worksheet. Your class may want to add a few encouraging or discouraging messages of their own. Then divide the class in half. Ask one half to write a story about a little boy or girl who constantly heard the negative messages. They should include how they felt and what happened to the child as he or she got older. The other half of the class will follow the same instructions, only they will write about a boy or girl who heard only positive messages. Once the students have finished their assignments, ask them to share their stories with the class and discuss how these tales relate to their own lives. Your students may find themselves developing new opinions towards listening once they understand where their negative feelings come from!

LEARNING WITH OTHERS

CHILDREN SHOULD BE HEARD

Read the discouraging and encouraging messages below. Add a few messages in both categories if you choose. Then with your teacher's help, write a story about a person, boy or girl, who only heard one category of these messages. What would happen to a boy or girl who only heard discouraging messages? What would happen to a boy or girl who only heard encouraging messages?

DISCOURAGING MESSAGES

"Be quiet."
"Hush."
"Shut up."
"Don't speak unless you are spoken to."
"Children should be seen but not heard."
"Don't talk back to me!"
"Who do you think you are talking like that?"
"Don't interrupt me while I'm talking."
"Open up those ears."
"Look at me when I talk to you."
"Why can't you pay better attention?"
"Hello . . . wake up . . . pay attention."

_____

_____

_____

ENCOURAGING MESSAGES

"If you can wait for a minute, I'd be happy to listen to what you have to say."

"I'd appreciate you hearing me out, then I'll listen to your thoughts and feelings."

"I like when you listen to me."

"Thank you for listening."

"I value your opinions, even if I don't agree with them."

"Could you lower your voice?"

_____

_____

_____

52

TELEPHONE

GOAL: Students will learn how easy it is for communications to become changed when they are exchanged by a large number of communicators.

TIME: 15 minutes

SETTING: classroom

PROCEDURE:

This is a classic activity that your students will enjoy. To prove to your students how important careful listening is, ask them to arrange themselves in a circle. Choose one student to be the first "operator." Whisper a silly phrase in his or her ear such as, "I saw our principal playing on the monkey bars this morning." The first operator must turn to the second operator and repeat whatever he or she heard. No repeats! The second operator turns to the third and so on. When the message finally reaches the last operator, it will undoubtedly be garbled. The last operator, then tells the class aloud what they heard. Your students are sure to have a good laugh when you repeat the original message.

Once the laughter dies down, point out that this activity demonstrates how information changes when not heard correctly. Have students brainstorm why the communication lines went down. Did the last operator mumble? Talk too soft? Talk too fast? Did other noises distract their attention? Did they change the message so it would make sense? Did they have to guess what was said in order to pass some message along? All of these interferences prevent good communication. Obviously, a lot of misunderstanding can occur when someone's not listening!

Name _____

BODY TALK

You are capable of communicating a lot without ever opening your mouth. Look at the pictures below and decide what each person is "saying." Once you have written all of your answers, compare your interpretations with your classmates.

Name _____

So What Are You "Saying"?

Almost every action we make communicates something about us. When you wake up in the morning for school, you are telling people that you find school important enough to go to! The clothes you chose for the day may also indicate how you are feeling. In the last activity, you learned that your facial expressions and body language can communicate your feelings. Look at the pictures below and decide what you think each student is "saying" about his personality, depending upon the outfit he is wearing.

_____

_____

_____

_____

_____

_____

When you finish writing, share your feelings about these boys with your class. You may also want to discuss whether you can really know a person just by looking at their clothes.

What's Wrong with This Picture?

Now that you're a communication "expert," see if you can detect what is wrong with each picture. Below each cartoon, write a sentence explaining how the listener could improve his or her listening skills.

Scene 1

I got in trouble today at school, Mom.

Oh, honey, that's great!

Scene 2

I was angry that I got in trouble because it wasn't my fault.

Mmmm, that's nice, dear.

Scene 1

Look, I got an A on my test!

What time is recess?

Scene 2

My dad will be the next President of the United States.

I can't wait to play kickball!

Scene 1

I'm worried about trying out for the soccer team today.

I wonder if I look good today?

Scene 2

I really hope I make the team!

Does he think I'm smart?

Oh! Good luck!

Scene 1

I'm frustrated with this math problem.

Oh, it's easy!

Scene 2

But I don't understand!

Just do it step by step as I showed you.

Name _____

DEFINITELY A DIFFERENCE IN DEFINITIONS

Have you ever noticed how some people use words differently than you do? If you want to effectively communicate with another person, you have to understand how they use words. And that's a big task considering how many people and how many words we will encounter in our lifetime! For this activity, you will need a partner, a pencil and a dictionary. Read each sentence. Write your interpretation of the italicized word, then switch papers with your partner and have them write their interpretation of the word. Finally, record each word's definition according to your dictionary. There's definitely a difference in definitions.

He *yelled* at me.
My Definition: _____
Partner's Definition: _____
Dictionary's Definition: _____

That movie was *radical*!
My Definition: _____
Partner's Definition: _____
Dictionary's Definition: _____

Help him with that assignment.
My Definition: _____
Partner's Definition: _____
Dictionary's Definition: _____

That's a hard *problem* to solve.
My Definition: _____
Partner's Definition: _____
Dictionary's Definition: _____

I *love* you.
My Definition: _____
Partner's Definition: _____
Dictionary's Definition: _____

You're *hurting* me.
My Definition: _____
Partner's Definition: _____
Dictionary's Definition: _____

Can I *borrow* a piece of paper?
My Definition: _____
Partner's Definition: _____
Dictionary's Definition: _____

FACT OR OPINION?

Sometimes we make judgements about another person's actions which are not accurate. We interpret their behavior through our opinions. Imagine a baby crying. Is the baby mad? Hungry? In need of attention? Trying out his or her lungs? When we add our interpretations or opinions about a situation, we sometimes misunderstand how the other person is thinking or feeling. Let's see how good you are at separating what is fact about each situation from what is the listener's opinion. This will help you become an unbiased listener. Circle the words in each sentence that are not a fact. Then share your work with your class.

1. José impatiently waited in line for his teacher to correct his paper.

2. Patricia slammed the door shut.

3. Elizabeth looked dreamily out the window as she sharpened her pencil.

4. Christian walked lazily down the hall.

5. Mr. Olive yells all the time because he is a mean teacher.

6. The tired little boy cried.

7. Verasol ate quickly because the food tasted good.

8. Calvin writes sloppily because he is a lazy student.

9. Brenda chews her gum loudly to annoy everyone.

10. Antonio jumped out of his chair because he was excited.

11. Manuel doesn't need anyone's help because he is so smart.

12. Candace is forgetful since she left her homework at home.

TLC10081 Copyright © Teaching & Learning Company, Carthage, IL 62321-0010

Name _____

Distractions All Around

Just as how we feel can effect our ability to listen, so can our surroundings. Look at the picture below. See how many external distractions you can identify by circling each one. Then discuss the distractions with your classmates. The next time you have difficulty listening to your teacher, look around the classroom and identify the distraction. Then you can suggest that your teacher eliminate the distraction so the students all around you can better listen, pay attention and learn!

I Can See Clearly Now . . .

GOAL: Students will understand how to ask questions that help to clarify what the speaker is attempting to communicate.

TIME: 45 minutes

SETTING: classroom

MATERIALS: worksheet on page 61

PROCEDURE:

Sometimes speakers have a clear idea in their head, but they do not effectively communicate the idea to the listener. When this happens, it's the listener's job to clarify what the speaker means. The listener wants to get as clear a picture as possible so that he or she will have the best understanding possible. This activity will help your students ask clarifying questions.

First, choose two students to role-play the "speaker" and the "listener." The rest of the class will need an "I Can See Clearly Now" worksheet. The speaker is going to read the first line of the dialogue below. After the speaker talks, the class is going to draw a picture of what they think the speaker is saying in Box 1. Give your students three to four minutes to do this. Once everyone has drawn their picture, the listener is going to ask the clarifying question below. After the speaker responds, the class will draw what they now think the speaker is saying in Box 2 and so on. Make sure the listener gives the class time to draw before helping the speaker clarify his or her statement!

Speaker: I bought a toy yesterday.
  (Pause three to four minutes.)

Listener: What kind of toy?

Speaker: A stuffed dog. (Pause three to four minutes.)

Listener: What kind of dog?

Speaker: A dalmatian. (Pause three to four minutes.)

Listener: Is it big or little?

Speaker: Big. (Pause three to four minutes.)

At the end of this exercise, ask your class, "If the speaker wanted to be understood the first time, what should he or she have said?" Your class should respond after all that drawing, "It would have been much easier if the speaker had said, 'I bought a big stuffed toy dalmatian yesterday.'" Hopefully, your students will see clearly now!

Name _____

I Can See Clearly Now . . .

You are going to listen to a conversation between a "speaker" and a "listener." Each time after the speaker talks, draw a picture of what you think they are talking about. Since the speaker is NOT clearly communicating the picture or idea in their head, the listener is going to help you by asking a clarifying question. Hopefully, with a little help from the clarifying questions, you'll be able to clearly see what the speaker is talking about by the end of this activity!

Box 1	**Box 2**
Box 3	**Box 4**

WE'RE ALL EARS

GOAL: Working in cooperative groups, students will improve and reflect on their listening skills in this fun problem-solving game.

TIME: 30 minutes

SETTING: classroom

MATERIALS: paper, pencil, three-column score sheet (snake, ear of corn, human ear)

PROCEDURE:

Did you ever notice how students often tune out important information? While the ability to turn off listening is a necessary skill in certain situations, students can strengthen their listening skills with practice. Here's a game to help you do just that.

Before you begin, you will need to select scorekeepers. Scorekeepers will be those students who have exhibited good listening skills in the past. The scorekeepers will not play in the game, they will be impartial observers, objectively keeping score for each team. To start the game, form student teams of five or six. Assign a student scorekeeper to each team.

Next, challenge the students to follow a set of directions *perfectly*. Let students know that for every direction listened to and acted on, points are earned. The team with the highest point total after the last direction is given will have the privilege of making up the directions for the next game to be played on another day.

Student scorekeepers will monitor team progress with a tally sheet: Partial Listening is rewarded with one point or a check in the "Ear of Corn" column; Perfect Listening is rewarded with two points and a check in the "Human Ear" column; and Failure to Listen will be penalized by placing a check in the "Snake" column, indicating no points will be earned. In case you're wondering–snakes have no ears! When a team gets three checks in the "Snake" column, they're out of the game.

When teams are formed and scorekeepers are ready with their score sheets, you are ready to start the game. Say to your students, "I will read you a series of directions that you should follow until the game is over. At the end of the game, the scorekeepers will add up the score for each team and present the score sheets to me. Ready?"

DIRECTIONS

1. Without talking, get in line from tallest to shortest.
2. While staying in line, form the letter *L* as a group.
3. Second person, put your hands on your knees.
4. Last person, face the opposite direction from the rest of the line.
5. Third person, put your arms out as if they are wings.
6. All people in line, put your right foot right in front of your left foot.
7. First person, look up.
8. Second from the last person, look down.
9. All members, make hands into fists.
10. All members, close one or both eyes.

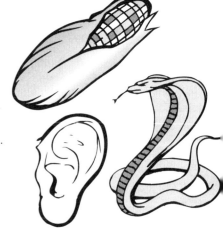

Option: You may want to let the scorekeepers see the directions before the game is played and even try the directions out so that they will know how to score their team. Scorekeepers can be held accountable for explaining how they scored their team if there are any disputes.

Name _____

We're All Ears

 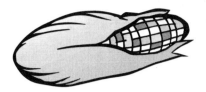

Let's see which team listens and follows directions the best. Scorekeepers you'll have to know your job. Make sure you watch to see if everyone on the team is following directions. If they are, then they earn one point in the "Human Ear" column. If someone on the team didn't listen and follow directions perfectly, then the team earns one point in the "Ear of Corn" column. And if no one on the whole team listened to or followed directions, then put a tally mark in the "Snake" column. By the way, if you didn't already know it, snakes have no ears!

Scorekeeper: _____

Team Players:

_____   _____   _____

_____   _____   _____

SNAKE   **EAR OF CORN**   **HUMAN EAR**

Add up the tally marks in each column. For each tally mark recorded in the Snake column, award zero points. For each tally mark recorded in the Ear of Corn column, award one point. And for each tally mark recorded in the Human Ear column, award two points. Add up the total points.

Total points: _____

LEARNING WITH OTHERS

WALK A MILE IN MY SHOES

GOAL: Students will experience empathy by putting themselves in another's shoes.

TIME: 40 minutes

SETTING: classroom

MATERIALS: "Shoe Shopping Spree" and "Walk a Mile in My Shoes" worksheets, blank paper, pencils, scissors, glue, crayons or markers

PROCEDURE:

Empathy takes a willingness to put yourself in another's shoes, so to speak. To begin, tell your students that each of them will select an imaginary pair of shoes to wear for the duration of the activity. In other words, your students will assume the identity of a person they believe would wear the shoes they selected.

Pass out one "Shoe Shopping Spree" worksheet to teams or tables of four to six students. Instruct your students to select and cut out only one pair of shoes. Everyone at the table should have a different pair of shoes. Encourage your students to choose the pair that they would be least likely to wear. Give your students a few minutes to color their shoes; this will help them settle into their new identity–to wear in their new shoes!

Now pass out a "Walk a Mile in My Shoes Reflection Sheet" to each student. Ask students to place their new shoes at the top of their "Reflection Sheet" and begin answering the questions. Encourage students to discuss their answers with their tablemates.

Once students have completed filling out the "Reflection Sheets," they can glue their shoes at the bottom of a blank piece of paper and draw the body and head of the person they created from the shoes up.

Name _____

SHOE SHOPPING SPREE

Name _____

WALK A MILE IN MY SHOES
REFLECTION SHEET

LEARNING WITH OTHERS

When we use empathy to understand someone, it is as if we are walking in the person's shoes–trying to see and experience the world as another does. In this activity your job is to become the character who wears the shoes you've selected. What do you think a person who wears the shoes is like? How would the person look? What does the person do? How does the person feel?

1. You have just selected a pair of shoes. Use your imagination and describe the kind of person who might wear these shoes.

   _____

   _____

2. If you were really in the shoes you selected, how would you feel about being outside in a rainstorm? Why?

   _____

   _____

3. Pretend that you are walking in a big city next to tall buildings, beautiful stores and fancy cars. Do you feel you belong here? Why?

   _____

   _____

4. As you walk, you pass someone who looks like she hasn't had a bath for a week. She asks you for something to eat. What would you do?

   _____

   _____

5. You are hungry now. It's nearly lunchtime. You take something out of your bag. What is it?

   _____

   _____

6. Thinking about your walk, where would you go right now? What will you do when you get there?

   _____

   _____

7. Did your thoughts and feelings about the person change as you played the game? How so?

   _____

   _____

8. How did the person become the way he or she is?

   _____

   _____

9. Now that you've walked a mile in these shoes, on another piece of paper draw a picture of the person. Start by pasting the shoes at the bottom of the page. Add legs, arms, a body and a face.

66

Literature in Support of Learning with Others

Alison's Zinnia by Anita Lobel (Greenwillow), 1990

The Candy Corn Contest by Patricia R. Giff (Dell), 1984

A Chair for My Mother by Vera B. Williams (Greenwillow), 1982

Charlie Anderson by Barbara Abercrombie (Simon & Schuster), 1990

Cherries and Cherry Pits by Vera B. Williams (Greenwillow), 1986

Chicken Sunday by Patricia Polacco (Putnam), 1992

The Christmas Carol by Charles Dickens (many editions)

A Cloak for the Dreamer by Aileen Friedman (Scholastic), 1995

Communication by Aliki (Greenwillow), 1993

The Cricket in Times Square by George Selden (Farrar, Straus & Giroux), 1960

Dove's Letter by Keith Baker (Harcourt, Brace & Co.), 1993

Down at Angel's by Sharon Chmielarz (Ticknor and Fields), 1984

A Fish in His Pocket by Denys Cazet (Orchard Books/Watts), 1987

Geraldine's Baby Brother by Holly Keller (Greenwillow), 1994

The Giving Tree by Shel Silverstein (Harper), 1994

The Good Bird by Peter Wezel (Harper), 1964

Good Griselle by Jane Yolen (Harcourt, Brace & Co.), 1994

The Great Pumpkin Switch by Megan McDonald (Orchard), 1995

The Great Smith House Hustle by Jane L. Curry (Simon & Schuster), 1993

The Hundred-Penny Box by Sharon B. Mathis (Puffin), 1986

King of Kings by Susan Hill (Candlewick Press), 1993

Littlejim's Gift: An Appalachian Christmas Story by Eloise McGraw (Putnam), 1994

Miss Tizzy by Libba M. Gray (Simon & Schuster), 1993

Mrs. Katz and Tush by Patricia Polacco (Dell), 1994

My Sister Celia by Judith Caseley (Greenwillow), 1986

Parents by Carme Sole Vendrell (Childrens Press), 1987

Poppa's New Pants by Angela S. Medearis (Holiday House), 1995

Prize in the Snow by Bill Easterling (Little), 1994

Quake! by Joe Cottonwood (Scholastic/Hardcover), 1995

The Real-Skin Rubber Monster Mask by Miriam Cohen (Greenwillow), 1990

Saying Good-Bye to Grandma by Jane R. Thomas (Houghton Mifflin Co.), 1990

Stefan & Olga by Betsy Day (Dial), 1991

There's a Dragon in My Sleeping Bag by James Howe (Atheneum), 1994

Tilly and the Rhinoceros by Sheila W. Samton (Putnam), 1993

Vegetable Soup by Jeanne Modesitt (Simon & Schuster), 1991

Wilson Sat Alone by Debra Hess (Simon & Schuster), 1994

SHARING FEELINGS
EXPRESSING EMOTIONS

One learns people through the heart, not the eyes or the intellect.

–Mark Twain

Imagine your students have a strong sense of self-control and were able to withstand emotional storms. What do you think your classroom would be like–calm, conflict free, productive? Self-mastery has been praised as virtue since the time of the ancient Greeks. The word they gave for it was *sphrosyne,* which means "care and intelligence in conducting one's life, a tempered balance."

These qualities come not from suppressing emotions but rather from gauging the appropriate amount of emotion and feeling in proportion to the circumstance. A life without feelings would be cold and desolate, not very rich, wouldn't you agree? When emotions are muffled, they create dullness and distance. On the other hand, when emotions are persistently out of control, they become pathological–often creating depression, overwhelming anxiety, raging anger and manic agitation.

Keeping our distressing emotions in check is the key to emotional well being. When distressing feelings are too intense or go on for too long, they can undermine our stability. Much of our behavior is an attempt to manage our moods. Everything, from reading a book or watching television, to the activities and friends we choose can be ways to make ourselves feel better. The art of soothing ourselves is a necessary component of healthy living.

To the degree that our students' emotions get in the way of or enhance their ability to think, plan or solve problems, defines their capacity to use their innate mental abilities. Their ability to regulate their emotions determines how they preform in your classroom and in life. Conversely, when our students are motivated by feelings of enthusiasm and pleasure for what they do, they are catapulted to success.

Those students who can tunc themselves to their own heart's voice–the language of emotion–will become more adept in articulating its messages. Teach your students to share their feelings appropriately.

SHARING FEELINGS THEME OBJECTIVES

1. PROVIDE OPPORTUNITIES TO DISCOVER PERSONAL COMMUNICATION STYLES

To become effective communicators, students need to look closely at themselves and others. We want our students to take a look at some of the patterns in their lives. We want them to approach interpersonal relationships from a scientific frame of mind. Our students will need to understand themselves and their impact on others so that they can manage relationships more effectively. And we want to help them understand those communication styles that are different from their own so that they can work productively with others rather than conflicting with them.

2. PROVIDE OPPORTUNITIES TO IDENTIFY AND APPROPRIATELY EXPRESS FEELINGS

Remember, we want to teach our students to express themselves from the heart as well as the head. Many of our students have been taught to hide their emotions and feelings. Unfortunately, this can make communication difficult for some. But, if our students are to move toward a state of emotional understanding, they will begin to know each other better when they share their feelings and emotions rather than merely expressing ideas about a situation. Keep in mind however that sharing feelings can lead to a sense of vulnerability. So make sure you take steps to keep the communications safe and trustful.

3. RECOGNIZE BEHAVIORAL STYLES: AGGRESSIVE, PASSIVE AND ASSERTIVE

It is important to know the difference between aggressive, passive and assertive behavior. Aggressive students will have a tendency to overreact to situations, blame or criticize others and may even physically attack one another. They also have very little consideration of the rights of others. Passive students will do things they do not want to do or make up lame excuses, instead of tell people how they really feel. They often lose a sense of self. Assertive students have learned to say what they think and stand up for what they believe without doing any harm to others. Teach your students the differences between these three communication behaviors.

FEELINGS

GOAL: Students will identify and appropriately express their feelings.

TIME: 25 minutes

SETTING: classroom

MATERIALS: "Feelings" worksheet, pencil

PROCEDURE:

Sometimes students have difficulty describing their emotions. Many times the difficulty arises from a lack of appropriate words to use when expressing their feelings. One sure-fire way of helping your students to express their feelings is to increase their vocabulary. Have your students use the "Feelings" worksheet in conjunction with a thesaurus to expand their vocabulary. Here's a partial list of feeling words for each category.

SAD	HAPPY	ANGRY	AFRAID
depressed	glad	annoyed	uneasy
confused	pleased	bothered	tense
bored	amused	bugged	concerned
resigned	contented	peeved	anxious
disappointed	comfortable	irritated	apprehensive
discontented	surprised	disgusted	worried
apathetic	relieved	harassed	alarmed
hurt	confident	resentful	shook
discouraged	cheerful	mad	threatened
drained	delighted	put upon	scared
distressed	up	set up	frightened
down	elated	contempt	panicky
unhappy	joyful	hate	overwhelmed
burdened	hopeful	hostile	petrified
miserable	eager	hot	terrified
ashamed	anticipating	burned	terror-stricken
crushed	great	furious	
humiliated	excited		
hopeless	enthusiastic		
despair	turned on		
anguish	moved		

If you'd like to extend this activity, have students write each feeling word on a 3" x 5" (8 x 13 cm) card. Then see if they can sort the cards into the appropriate categories (sad, happy, angry, afraid). They'll love this activity as a center or a game!

Name _____

FEELINGS

Sometimes it's hard to know exactly how you're feeling and how to express what you feel. One way to improve your communication skills is by increasing your feeling vocabulary so you can better describe what mood you're in. See how many synonyms and associated words you can list for each feeling word below. A thesaurus is a great resource for this activity!

SAD	HAPPY	ANGRY	AFRAID

_____   _____   _____   _____

_____   _____   _____   _____

_____   _____   _____   _____

_____   _____   _____   _____

_____   _____   _____   _____

_____   _____   _____   _____

_____   _____   _____   _____

_____   _____   _____   _____

_____   _____   _____   _____

CORNERS

GOAL:	Students will identify and appropriately express feelings.
TIME:	25 minutes
SETTING:	classroom
MATERIALS:	four pieces of 8½" x 11" (21 x 28 cm) paper, scrap paper

PROCEDURE:

Most elementary school children are just beginning to recognize their feelings. Often their thoughts and feelings are based on their friends' and family's thoughts and feelings. This activity should help your students make individual choices about their own preferences.

Before the lesson, select four categories for your students to choose from. For example, four animals such as a tiger, an elephant, a monkey and an ostrich or four types of boats such as a sailboat, a motorboat, a rowboat and an ocean liner. Write one category on each piece of 8½" x 11" (21 x 28 cm) paper. Post one category in each of the four corners of your room.

Now you're ready to begin the lesson. Explain to your students that they are going to look at the four corners of the room and decide which category they identify with the most. Give them one minute to write their choice on a piece of scrap paper. Do not allow them to confer with their friends. Ask your students to walk to the category they have chosen. Once they are in their respective corners, ask them to find a partner. They are now going to tell their partner why they chose that corner. For example, one student may choose the tiger because it runs the fastest, another student may choose the monkey because it clowns around the most. Once the partners have shared their reasons, have each group choose a Spokesperson. The Spokesperson will poll the group to determine the most common reasons for choosing the corner. Have the groups share their reasons with the class. Then have your students return to their seats.

Conduct a class discussion about corners. Your class might discuss:
- What new things did you learn about people in our class?
- Was it hard or easy to choose a corner? Why or why not?
- How did you feel when you shared your reasons? Why?
- Did you want to change your choice once you saw what your friends chose? Why or why not?

Donning a New Hat

GOAL: Students will learn assertion skills.

TIME: one hour

SETTING: classroom

MATERIALS: Three hats per group, "Meet Ima!" worksheet, scissors, tape or pins, "Story-Cards," "My Communication Style Assessment Worksheet," pencils

PROCEDURE:

As your students have learned, people communicate by using more than just words. What they say conveys only one part of the message. How your students say the words combined with their actions sends the listener a comprehensive communication package. Over time, people develop communication patterns and styles. One way of classifying communication styles is by dividing people's words and actions into three categories: Aggressive, Passive and Assertive. This activity will allow students to experience what it feels like to respond to different situations in all three communication styles. To prepare for the activity, each student will need to bring a hat that they can share with the class.

Before your students can begin the experiential part of this activity, they must understand the three communication styles. Divide your class into groups of four. Then give each group the "Meet Ima!" worksheet so they can refer to the three categories when they begin their activity. Teach a directed lesson using the description below and the worksheet as a guide.

The "Meet Ima!" worksheet describes Ima, a little girl who can communicate using all three styles. When Ima is feeling self-confident, honest and direct, she communicates assertively. She respects other people's opinions, yet she ultimately makes her own decisions. She feels responsible for her own behavior. You'll often hear *Ima Sertive* say, "Let's talk about this some more. Then I'll need some time to think about it and to make my own decision."

Ima Mouse is quieter. She easily gives in to other people's wishes. She usually cannot make up her own mind when confronted with a situation so she often does nothing. She does not communicate how she truly feels. Sometimes she gets angry when her ideas are not heard. If you hang out with Ima Mouse, you'll hear her say, "I don't know. Just have it your way. What's the difference anyway? I don't care."

When you run into *Ima Brute*, watch out! She's likely to tell you exactly what she thinks and feels without considering your thoughts or feelings. She is direct and sometimes hostile. She believes that her ideas are the best. In short, she has an attitude. *Ima Brute* is most likely to say, "Don't tell me what to do! I'll do whatever I want."

Now tell your students that they are going to role-play several situations tomorrow using Ima's three communication styles. If needed, review the three different facets of Ima's communication styles to make sure that students understand the differences between assertive, passive and aggressive. Have children sit in a circle within their groups. Next, they should decide who is going to start as "Ima Sertive," "Ima Mouse," "Ima Brute" and as the Storyteller. Have them cut out, then tape or pin the appropriate picture of "Ima" onto their hat. The Storyteller can tape or pin that title onto their hat.

Next, distribute the Story Cards to the Storytellers. The Storyteller is going to read the story to his or her group and then ask each of the "Imas" to respond in "her" typical fashion. Give your students several minutes to read and respond to the story. Now pass out the "My Communication Style Assessment" worksheet. Have the "Imas" write how they felt role playing their communication style on the appropriate lines. (The Storyteller will not write anything.) Then ask your students to put a check in the box that represents how they would typically respond (as themselves) at the bottom of the page. For example, if they feel that they would say something similar to what "Ima Mouse" said, then they should put their check in the Passive box for Story 1.

Have your students take off their "Ima" hats and pass their hat to their left. The new Storyteller will read the second story and the new "Imas" will respond according to their new character. Again after your students have had a chance to role-play, ask them to record their feelings on their assessment worksheet. Repeat this process two more times so every student within the group has acted out each role (Ima Sertive, Ima Mouse, Ima Brute and the Storyteller).

Finally, have a class discussion about which communication style felt most comfortable for your students. Hopefully your students will recognize that Ima Sertive is mostly likely to be true to herself while not offending others!

Name _____

DONNING A NEW HAT
MEET IMA!

Hi there! We'd like you to meet Ima, a little girl who can communicate using all three communication styles. Sometimes Ima feels assertive, other times she acts passively and once in a while she's aggressive. Pay attention to how Ima speaks so you can effectively role-play each Ima for the next activity.

Ima Sertive is assertive. When Ima is feeling self-confident, honest and direct, she communicates assertively. She respects other people's opinions, yet she ultimately makes her own decisions. She feels responsible for her own behavior.

Ima Mouse is passive. She is quieter. She easily gives in to other people's wishes. She usually cannot make up her own mind when confronted with a situation so she often does nothing. She does not communicate how she truly feels. Sometimes she gets angry when her ideas are not heard.

Ima Brute is aggressive. When you run into Ima Brute, watch out! She's likely to tell you exactly what she thinks and feels without considering your thoughts or feelings. She is direct and sometimes hostile. She believes that her ideas are the best and don't dare tell her otherwise. In short, she has an attitude.

STORYTELLER
DONNING A NEW HAT
STORY CARDS

STORY 1

Your teacher assigned a project with the option to work in pairs. You and your friend Alfonso decide to work together. Alfonso fools around whenever the two of you are working on your project at each other's homes. On the night before it's due, he offers to put on the finishing touches. The following day, he turns in the project with only his name on it. Your teacher says, "Alfonso, what a great job!" He doesn't say that you worked together. How would you respond?

STORY 2

You are the president of your school's Student Council. Your advisor has encouraged you to organize some school-wide activities. Everyone on Student Council is excited about having a school carnival. When you ask your principal, she says that it will never work. How do you respond?

STORY 3

Your little brother loves to get you in trouble then play innocent. After school, he took a box of cereal and dumped it all over the kitchen. When your father gets home, he demands to know who made the mess. Your little brother immediately says that you did it and made it look like something you would do to get him in trouble. You protest, but your father says that you're older and even if you didn't do it, you should have stopped him. How do you respond?

STORY 4

Kimberly, the most popular girl in the class is having a boys' and girls' birthday party this weekend. Everyone has been talking about it at school. Kimberly says that everyone is invited if they promise to play Truth or Dare. You want to go to the party, but you don't want to play the game. In front of all your friends, Kimberly asks you if you're willing to promise. When you hesitate, she says, "What's the matter, baby, are you chicken?" How do you respond?

Name _____

DONNING A NEW HAT
MY COMMUNICATION STYLE ASSESSMENT

Complete the appropriate part of this worksheet after you respond to each story.

When I was "Ima Sertive," my response was . . .

_____

_____

When I responded assertively, I felt . . .

_____

_____

When I was "Ima Mouse," my response was . . .

_____

_____

When I responded passively, I felt . . .

_____

_____

When I was "Ima Brute," my response was . . .

_____

_____

When I responded aggressively, I felt . . .

_____

_____

My most typical response as myself would probably be . . .

	Assertive	Passive	Aggressive
Story 1:	❑	❑	❑
Story 2:	❑	❑	❑
Story 3:	❑	❑	❑
Story 4:	❑	❑	❑

FEELER REVEALER

GOAL: Students will cooperatively build their vocabulary as it pertains to three different emotional states: happy, angry and sad.

TIME: 30 minutes

SETTING: classroom

MATERIALS: three "Feeler Revealer" worksheets for each group of four to six students and three large pieces of butcher paper for clustering

PROCEDURE:

Have you ever noticed that when it comes to feelings, people say different things? When talking with your students about feelings, it's important that everyone have some common definitions.

To start this activity, organize students into cooperative groups of four to six. Once students are situated in their groups, explain that "We all have different definitions and understandings of words. Now it's time we put our heads together to come up with meanings of synonyms for feeling words that we can all agree on and use. This way we will really understand how a person feels when they are sad, angry or even happy."

Next, explain the "Feeling Revealer" worksheets to students. Point out that the first column, "In Other Words," will help us to explain what each feeling means. Each group will have to work together to provide words that are synonyms for the feeling word. The second column, "What Causes Me to Feel This Way?" will help us to explain the different reasons for each feeling. This column will be a list of words or situations that people in your group have experienced.

Now distribute three "Feeler Revealer" worksheets to each group. Say to your students, "Each group has three copies of the "Feeler Revealer" worksheets. In the first column I'd like you to write what you think the word at the top of the sheet means. Try to write as many other words that mean the same thing in this column. For example, if the word on the top of your sheet is *happy*, you can write the words *glad*, *proud of myself*, *full of energy* and *smiley* in the first column." Write these words on the chalkboard and give students a chance to write a few words on their sheets.

Continue explaining the activity by saying, "In the second column, you can write things that make you feel happy such as when you buy a toy or get an A on a test." Write these examples on the chalkboard.

Give students approximately five minutes to fill in each sheet calling the time after each five-minute period passes. Then facilitate a class conversation in which students' discuss their worksheets and their definition variations or synonyms. Record your students' answers on a large sheet of butcher paper so that everyone will be able understand clearly what is meant when a student feels sad, angry or happy.

To conclude the Feeler Revealer activity, compliment your students on their examples and how they worked together. Tell them that cooperation like this makes you happy. They will have a keener understanding of what you mean.

Name _____

FEELER REVEALER

Everybody has feelings, right? Of course they do! Sometimes people express their feelings freely, and other times people hide their feelings from others. Sometimes feeling words mean the same to everybody, and other times those feeling words mean different things to different people. Sometimes people feel one particular feeling for the same reasons, other times people feel the same feeling for different reasons. Now is the time for all of us to better understand each other's feelings. Take the time to fill out the chart below and if you feel comfortable, you can reveal your feeling words with others in your class.

Choose a feeling:

Happy   **Sad**   **Angry**

Write your feeling word here: _____

In Other Words	What Causes Me to Feel This Way
_____	_____
_____	_____
_____	_____
_____	_____
_____	_____
_____	_____
_____	_____

FEELINGS THERMOMETER

GOAL: Students will demonstrate understanding of different feelings.

TIME: 20 minutes

SETTING: classroom

MATERIALS: "Feelings Thermometer Scenarios" and "Feelings Thermometer" worksheet for each student

PROCEDURE:

Now that you've had an opportunity to expand upon your students' use of the words *happy, angry* and *sad* in the Feeler Revealer activity, you'll want to help students identify particular feelings that would arise in response to certain possible scenarios. And once the feelings to the scenarios provided have been identified, students will also benefit from determining where they would rank those feelings from low to high, or hot to cold, on a continuum or "thermometer."

When a student becomes more capable of identifying their emotions, they become more self-aware. Many of the feelings students have are completely out of our students' awareness. We have all different types of emotions. Some emotions are protective in nature, such as: anger, sadness and fear. Other emotions are accusations or actually evaluations of self and others, such as: guilt, rejection, abandonment, resentment, anxiety and depression. And still other emotions are growth emotions, such as: love, happiness and trust.

The thermometer provided is labeled *Happiness–Love* at the high end of the thermometer and *Upset–Angry, Sad or Fearful* at the low end of the thermometer. Using the scenarios provided, instruct students to cut them apart and place them on the Feelings Thermometer. Advise students to try the characters in different places before pasting the descriptions. Lots of critical thinking will go on; don't fret about raucous conversation! Keep the conversation lively after thermometers are finished.

Name _____

FEELINGS THERMOMETER SCENARIOS

Put the names of each of these people on your Feelings Thermometer in order, from those who are *most* happy close to the happy end of the thermometer, and those *most* upset, sad or angry closest to the upset end of the thermometer. Then sort the other people somewhere in between—wherever you think they belong. Take a few minutes to do this quietly and then we'll discuss your answers.

 Tim: Just received a test paper with an F on it.

 **Denise:** Is enjoying a day at the park.

 Anna: Her grandmother died yesterday.

 **José:** Lost his favorite sneakers.

 Josh: Sits bored in front of the television.

 Trina: Found a kitten.

 Rosa: Someone cut in front of her in line.

 Julianne: Has waited 15 minutes for her mother to pick her up from school.

 Emmanuel: Got an award for most improved student in class.

 **Chris:** Wasn't chosen for the football team.

Name _____

FEELINGS THERMOMETER

HAPPINESS — LOVE

Now that you have had an opportunity to read over the situations provided, you'll want to organize them on this thermometer. How are you going to arrange them?

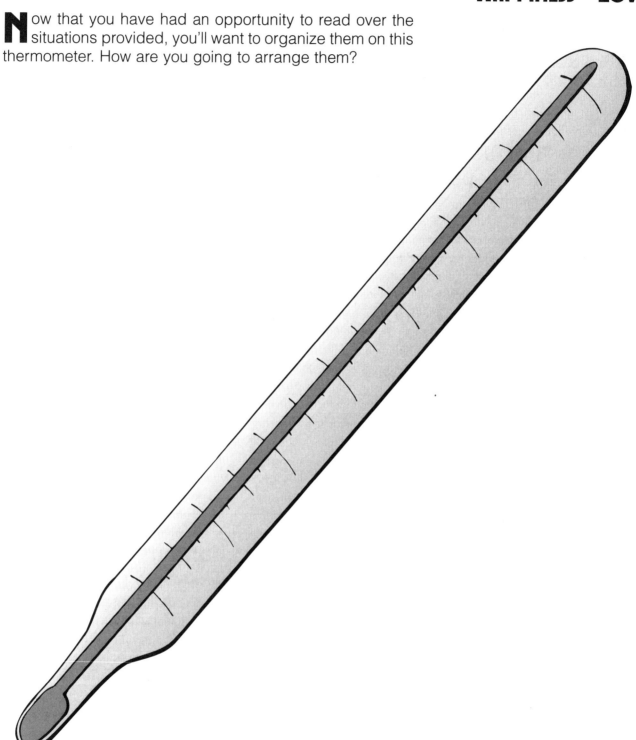

UPSET — ANGRY, SAD OR FEARFUL

FEELINGS FORECAST

GOAL: Students will learn to identify their emotional weather conditions in order to simply vent their feelings and seek support for themselves.

TIME: 40 minutes

SETTING: classroom

MATERIALS: class sets of the four feeling cards: happy, angry, sad and scared on page 85; six to 10 three-minute egg timers

PROCEDURE:

Here's a great activity to start your week. As students walk into the classroom on Monday morning, invite them to select a feeling necklace that best fits their mood and put it on. Make sure you explain that they should make their own decisions and choose either a happy, angry, sad or scared face. It's best if this decision-making process is done in a quiet environment. Allow students a few minutes to make their decisions.

Once your students have selected and put on a necklace, have them sit quietly at a table that has a table marker with the same face that they are wearing. Each group sitting at a particular "feeling table" should have no more than six people. If, for example, it happens to be a particularly blue Monday, you may need to have two groups of . . . well, you know what feeling.

When you try this the first time, there may be some confusion and more extraneous talking than ideal. So you may want to explain to students that this is an activity that you would like them to take seriously. You can say, "Our feelings are very fragile, and we must be very sensitive and caring to others when they are given a chance to talk. Nobody wants to show their feelings if they think others will laugh at them."

Now that the groups have been organized, you will want to explain the following: "Each person can take up to three minutes to explain how she came to feel the way she does. If you are having trouble expressing your feelings, you may pass your turn to the next person. But most of you should try to say something, if you can."

Assign one student from each group to be the timekeeper and instruct them to keep track of each participant's time with an egg timer. The other students in the group should practice attentive listening skills. After each person has had an opportunity to express themselves within each group, encourage students to find a communication partner for the day. The communication partners will agree to listen, when possible, to each other for a full day. Remember, listening is enough. Let students know that suggesting solutions to any personal problems that may be expressed is not necessary.

As this activity progresses and as your students have the opportunity to communicate and be heard, they may actually wish to reidentify themselves and change groups. If this is the case, please encourage them to do so.

Closing questions to ask your students:

1. Did you like this activity?
2. What did you notice about the people in your group?
3. Did you notice anything about the different groups? In what way did the groups communicate?
4. Which group had the most people in it? Why do you think more people were in that group than any other?
5. Did everyone in your feeling group communicate their feelings?
6. Why do you think it is harder for some people to explain their feelings than others?

FEELINGS FORECAST FACES

HAPPY

SAD

ANGRY

SCARED

Jivin' in the Jungle: Self-Assessment

GOAL: Students will discover their personal communication styles.

TIME: This is a five-part activity that can be done over several days. This section will take 30 to 60 minutes.

SETTING: classroom

MATERIALS: "Jivin' in the Jungle: Self-Assessment" worksheet, pencils

PROCEDURE:

You are the safari leader, about to take your class into a jungle. On this trip, each student is going to learn about their personal communication/behavioral style. They will have to listen to their leader's explanations, make assessments about their behavior, form groups and complete a task in order to return home safely.

In the jungle, you are going to encounter four animals, which are representative of four communication styles. After hearing the descriptions of each animal, your students are going to decide which animal they are most like. Caution your students against making hasty decisions! They should not choose their favorite animal, nor the animal they desire to be like, but rather the animal which most closely resembles their communication style. Some students may have difficulty deciding. You may have to assist with the decision. Other students may assert that they sometimes resemble one animal, while at other times they resemble another. Encourage these students to choose the animal they act like *most often*. Choosing one animal does not mean they are 100% similar to this animal, 100% of the time. All animals have both positive and negative qualities.

To help you better understand the correlation between the four communication/behavioral styles and the four animals, here's a summary of the characteristics of each style.

Lions can also be called **Drivers.** These students are assertive and self-controlled people. In a group setting, they like to get their way. They are task-oriented thinkers who know what they want to accomplish and how they are going to accomplish it. Rarely do they show their emotions. These students are experts at control; they can control a group while also controlling their emotions. Adjectives that describe Drivers include: *determined, thorough, decisive, efficient, dominating, pushy* and *tough-minded.*

Giraffes can also be called **Analyticals**. These students are not assertive but are good at controlling their emotions. They like to ask questions and gather facts so that they can, from their heightened viewpoint, see and understand all situations in their entirety. They are predominantly thinkers, not feelers. These students are technical experts; they are reserved and in control in group situations. Adjectives that describe Analyticals include: *industrious, persistent, serious, orderly, critical* and *indecisive.*

Monkeys can be called **Expressives**. These students are very aggressive and also very verbal about making their feelings known. They do not attempt to control their emotions, instead they react impulsively to many situations. They are more concerned about the people in a group than the task at hand. They will disregard facts if their gut tells them to. These rather chatty students are social experts because they combine personal power and emotional expression in their relationships. Adjectives that describe Expressives include: *personable, stimulating, enthusiastic, dramatic, manipulative, excitable* and *undisciplined.*

Chameleons can also be called **Amiables**. These students display their feelings openly but are not very assertive. They constantly change colors striving to be agreeable with most people. These students are experts in support; they are personally reserved and also capable of emotional expression to help others in their group. Adjectives that describe Amiables include: *supportive, respectful, willing, dependable, agreeable, dependent, conforming* and *emotional.*

Depending on your students' developmental level, you may want to further expand the animal metaphors by discussing the explanations given above.

Often people express a desire to work in groups in which everyone is like them. This activity will show students that having all one communication/behavioral style in one group may not be the most beneficial for the group. By recognizing each style, and the strengths and weaknesses that come with it, students will be better able to work together as an effective team. Now that you've been briefed on each style, you should be ready to lead your class on this safari adventure!

Before you describe each animal, pass out the "Jivin' in the Jungle: Self-Assessment" worksheet. Read the following explanation/story to your students. You will begin by describing the lion.

JIVIN' IN THE JUNGLE STORY

Tell students to close their eyes and imagine themselves at the edge of the jungle. Suddenly they see a lion race past, followed by several lion cubs. The lion looks very determined to get to the other side of the jungle. She does not stop to talk with any of the other animals who call out to her. The lion does not waste any time. When one of the cubs stops to check out the safari group that you are in, the lion gives a roar of disapproval and the cub immediately runs after. You can tell that the lion is used to getting her way around these cubs!

As the lion runs out of sight, you see a tall giraffe walking near the edge of the trees. The giraffe carefully looks at each leaf on each tree before deciding which one to eat. He considers each one thoughtfully before making his choice. Often you see him stretch his long neck to examine the rest of the jungle. You realize he must have a very good view of the jungle from way up there. Because he is so high, he can see danger from far away and decide the best plan of action for his safety. Once he has taken a good look around, he continues to eat. He examines each leaf in an orderly manner and then goes on to the next tree.

As the giraffe reaches for a leaf, suddenly a monkey bursts out of the branches. The monkey asks the giraffe, "How are you today?" As the giraffe thinks about how he will answer the monkey's question, the monkey sees some of her monkey friends and swings off to join them. The giraffe is just as happy that the monkey left; he didn't really want to share his feelings anyway.

Your safari group follows the monkey into the jungle. The monkey appears to be very excited! The monkey is swinging from branch to branch talking to all the animals she sees. Sometimes she makes faces at her monkey friends to put on a little show. Her mother calls her over to help her clean her little brother's coat, but she keeps getting distracted. She'd rather play with him, rather than get his coat as shiny as her mother likes it to be. Even better, she'd like to go talk to her friends! She can't wait to go tell her best friend about what she saw earlier today! Hmm . . . where is her best friend? Maybe the chameleon would know. He's always helpful!

The monkey jumps down to the jungle floor and spots the chameleon. The chameleon is a pretty green color, but as the monkey approaches, the chameleon changes to a brilliant red. Chameleon knows that red is the monkey's favorite color. Monkey asks if he's seen her best friend. You overhear the chameleon saying that he hasn't, but he wishes that he could help. He says that if he sees her, he'll let the monkey know. The chameleon's very dependable, so monkey races off to look elsewhere. The chameleon notices that two of the people in the safari group are crying because they are homesick. The chameleon changes to blue and wanders over to the group to see if he can be supportive. He respectfully asks if he can help. When the answer is "no," he agreeably leaves.

All of this animal watching is making you tired. Your safari leader suggests that everyone sit down in the clearing to take a break. You think that this is a great idea! Now you'll have time to think about everything you saw!

Now have students open their eyes. Ask them to keep each animal and its behavior in their minds as they follow the directions on the "Jivin' in the Jungle: Self-Assessment" worksheet.

Name _____

JIVIN' IN THE JUNGLE
SELF-ASSESSMENT

As you take a break from your safari, think about the animals you saw and how they behaved. Read the statements below each animal. Circle any statements that sound similar to how you usually act. Finally, put a star by the animal that you think is most similar to you.

Lion

I tell other people what I'm thinking.
I do not like to show my feelings.
I like other people to do what I say.
When I have a job to do, I get it done without wasting time.
If someone does something that I do not like,
        I tell them that I do not like it.
I have a lot of determination.

Giraffe

I like to ask a lot of questions and gather facts.
I think a lot before making a decision.
I do not like to share my feelings.
I am usually serious.
I like my belongings to be neat and orderly.
I work hard.

Monkey

I like to tell lots of people about my feelings.
I get very excited and enthusiastic easily.
I care about how people feel, not about getting a job done.
I like to talk, talk, talk.
I act on my feelings, not on my thoughts.
I like to play.

Chameleon

I hate it when people are mad at me.
I like to share my feelings.
I like to please other people.
I am dependable, responsible and respectful.
I like to be helpful.
I am happy when everyone around me is happy.

JIVIN' IN THE JUNGLE: CLASS ASSESSMENT

GOAL: Students will identify the personal communication styles of their classmates.

TIME: 45 minutes

SETTING: classroom

MATERIALS: "Jivin' in the Jungle: Class Assessment" worksheet, pencils, chalkboard, chalk

PROCEDURE:

Once each student has determined his or her personal communication/behavior style, you are ready for the next adventure on your safari! But first your class must form survival groups. Your class is going to perform an "experiment" to see how a group of all one animal type (i.e. communication style) works together.

To form the survival groups, write the names of all of your students on the chalkboard. Now, using the "Jivin' in the Jungle: Class Assessment" worksheet, ask your students to decide which animal each of their classmates most closely resembles. Students may have different opinions of how their classmates should be classified, but most likely there will be some agreement as to a particular classification.

Now that the students are done assessing each other's communication styles, you (as the safari leader) must compile the lists to form the groups. Write the four animals' names on the chalkboard. Begin with the first student listed on the chalkboard. Ask your students, "How many people think _____ is a lion? A giraffe? A monkey? A chameleon?" If there is a lack of consensus, ask students to support their statements with examples of the student in question's behavior, or ask the student for their self-assessment. You may need to be the final arbitrator. When all students have been "classified," ask each group to sit together to find out about their next adventure!

Name _____

JIVIN' IN THE JUNGLE
CLASS ASSESSMENT

For the next part of your safari, you are going to break up into groups. Think about the four kinds of animals and about your classmates. Under the name of each animal, write the names of your classmates that are similar to that animal. Your teacher will compile a class list.

LION

GIRAFFE

_____
_____
_____
_____
_____
_____
_____

_____
_____
_____
_____
_____
_____
_____

MONKEY

CHAMELEON

_____
_____
_____
_____
_____
_____
_____

_____
_____
_____
_____
_____
_____
_____

JIVIN' IN THE JUNGLE: THE ADVENTURE BEGINS

GOAL: Students will work in groups of like communication styles.

TIME: 60 minutes

SETTING: classroom

MATERIALS: "Jivin' in the Jungle: Adventure Worksheet"

PROCEDURE:

For the next part of your safari adventure, the survival groups are going to work together to complete a task. This task will provide an opportunity for your students to observe how people with the same communication/behavioral style work together. They may discover that having a group of all lions, all giraffes, all monkeys or all chameleons may not be the best way to complete a job. This activity should also show your students that every communication/behavioral style has its strengths and weaknesses. One style is not superior to the others.

So let the adventures begin! Pass out *one* "Jivin' in the Jungle: Adventure Worksheet" to each *group*. Tell the groups that they have 30 minutes to complete the sheet and solve the problems described. Observe the groups' interactions, but do NOT encourage the groups to stay on task. You may be able to provide some insight into their behavior that will be valuable during the Survival Group Assessment component of this activity. Some groups may not finish due to the communication style of their group.

When the half hour is over, ask students to reflect on their group's experience.

How did your group decide who should read the worksheet?
How did your group decide who should write on the worksheet?
Did your group finish the worksheet?
What helped your group to complete the worksheet?
What prevented your group from completing the worksheet?
Is everyone in your group satisfied with your group's solution?
Was your group supportive of each other's ideas? How or why not?

Name _____

Jivin' in the Jungle
Adventure Worksheet

Your safari leader has divided your safari into survival groups for your safety. The jungle can be a dangerous place! It's getting dark and you must find food and a place to camp for the night. Your safari leader has instructed the survival groups to split up so you can cover the most ground possible.

Your group knows its mission. You set off to look for food. Soon, you come to a river. You haven't found any food yet. Should you try to cross it? What's in the water? Are there dangerous animals lurking below the surface? What's on the other side? Too late! Your group is going to have to cross the river because a fire has started behind you. One of the other survival groups must have been careless when cooking their food. You can see by the smoke that you have 30 minutes before the fire gets to the river. How is your group going to cross the river? One of the people in your group is very afraid of water and cannot swim.

We decided to cross the river by . . .

_____

_____

_____

_____

Now that you are on the other side. You need to find food. You're hungry! How do you find the food? We found the food by . . .

_____

_____

_____

_____

Just as you start to eat, you see your safari leader with the other survival groups. You can't wait to tell them what happened to your group! But first listen to what your safari leader has to say.

JIVIN' IN THE JUNGLE: THE FINAL CHALLENGE

GOAL: Students will work in groups with different personal communication styles.

TIME: 60 minutes

SETTING: classroom

MATERIALS: "Jivin' in the Jungle: The Final Challenge" worksheet, pencils

PROCEDURE:

For the final leg of your safari, your class will work in groups comprised of different communication styles. This activity should demonstrate to students that when all communication styles work together–lions, monkeys, giraffes and chameleons–the result is an effective team. The lions should keep the team on task. The giraffes should examine all issues thoroughly. The monkeys should maintain enthusiasm. The chameleons should be supportive of all the members of the team. And as your students have experienced, "It's a jungle out there," so we all need to work together!

First, redesignate the survival teams. Make sure that each team has at least one lion, monkey, giraffe and chameleon, and that all teams have roughly the same number of members. Then distribute one "Jivin' in the Jungle: The Final Challenge" worksheet to each group. As the final challenge, your students will have to solve a problem to get out of the jungle alive. This time students will be writing a story–collectively. Each member on the team is responsible for two sentences. Allow students approximately one half hour to complete the activity. Remember, do not help or encourage the groups to stay on task!

Finally, conclude this lesson with a class discussion. First, use the same questions from the last activity as a comparison between groups composed of the same communication styles (see page 92) versus groups composed of different communication styles. Then ask these additional questions to help students further improve their communication skills.

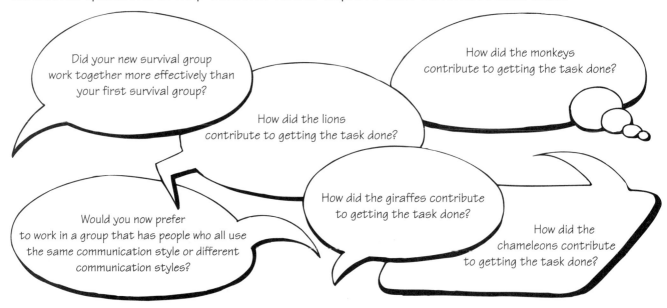

Did your new survival group work together more effectively than your first survival group?

How did the monkeys contribute to getting the task done?

How did the lions contribute to getting the task done?

How did the giraffes contribute to getting the task done?

How did the chameleons contribute to getting the task done?

Would you now prefer to work in a group that has people who all use the same communication style or different communication styles?

Jivin' in the Jungle
The Final Challenge

You were relieved to be with your safari leader in the dangerous jungle last night. You and your friends slept soundly. Now that it's morning, your safari leader has divided you into new teams–the team that you are working with now. Today is the final day of your safari. Your leader is going to make arrangements for the plane that will take you home. But before your leader leaves, she instructs you to clean up the camp and meet at the landing strip in four hours. Your leader stresses the importance of arriving on time. You have no more food. If your group fails to leave before sundown, you will not make your connecting flight home, which means you will be stuck in the jungle for another week. Your survival group does a good job clearing out of camp and then makes its way to the runway. The plane is there, but you do not see the pilot or your leader! Oh no!

Each person in your survival group must contribute two sentences to finish the safari story. Within the next half hour, your group must explain what happened to the pilot, your leader and how you work together to get out of the jungle by sundown. Are you up to the final challenge? Remember, the jungle is dangerous. Your life depends on it!

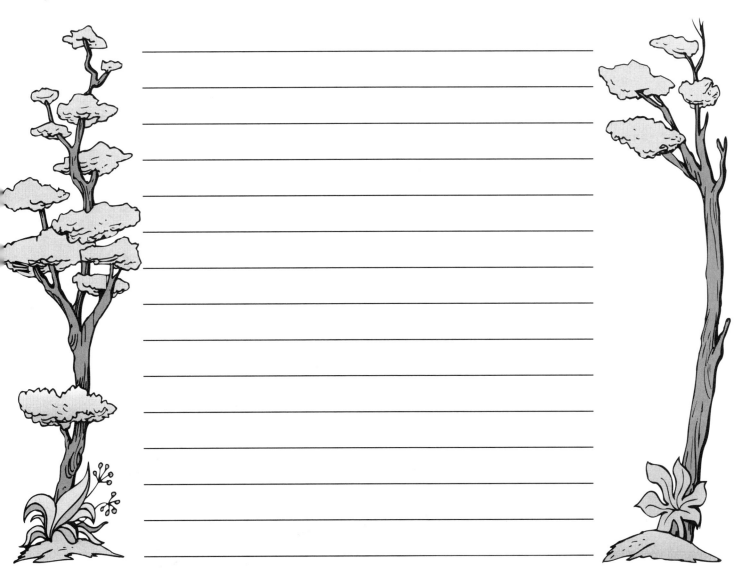

LITERATURE IN SUPPORT OF SHARING FEELINGS

Banner Year by Betty Cavanna (Morrow), 1987

Bootsie Barker Bites by Barbara Bottner (Putnam), 1992

Bringing the Farmhouse Home by Gloria Whelan (Simon & Schuster), 1992

A Color of His Own by Leo Lionni (Knopf), 1993

Communication by Aliki (Greenwillow), 1993

Crow Boy by Taro Yashima (Puffin Books), 1976

Definitely Cool by Brenda Wilkinson (Scholastic/Hardcover), 1993

Dove's Letter by Keith Baker (Harcourt, Brace & Co.), 1993

Fast Friends by Lisa Horstman (Knopf), 1994

Feel Better, Ernest! by Gabrielle Vincent (Greenwillow), 1988

Feelings by Aliki (Greenwillow), 1984

The Good-Night Kiss by Jim Aylesworth (Simon & Schuster), 1993

Grandmother & I by Helen E. Buckley (Lothrop), 1994

Harry & Willy & Carrothead by Judith Caseley (Greenwillow), 1991

How Do I Feel? by Norma Simon (Albert Whitman & Co.), 1970

I'm Terrific by Majorie W. Sharmat (Holiday House, Inc.), 1977

It's Perfectly Normal by Robie H. Harris (Candlewick Press), 1994

The Kids Book of Questions by Gregory Stock (Workman Publications), 1988

King of the Playground by Phyllis R. Naylor (Simon & Schuster), 1994

Learning by Heart by Ronder Y. Young (Houghton Mifflin Co.), 1993

Mr. Nick's Knitting by Margaret Wild (Harcourt, Brace & Co.), 1989

My Best Friend by Pat Hutchins (Greenwillow), 1993

The River That Gave Gifts by Margo Humphrey (Children's Press), 1995

Roommates by Kathryn O. Galbraith (Simon & Schuster), 1990

Saying Good-Bye to Grandma by Jane R. Thomas (Houghton Mifflin Co.), 1990

Shadow Boxer by Chris Lynch (HarperCollins), 1995

Someday by Charlotte Zolotow (HarperCollins), 1989

Someone New by Charlotte Zolotow (HarperCollins), 1978

Sophie and Lou by Petra Mathers (HarperCollins), 1991

There's a Nightmare in My Closet by Mercer Mayer (Puffin Books), 1992

The Tongue-Cut Sparrow by Momoko Ishii (Dutton), 1987

Too Many Murphys by Colleen O. McKenna (Scholastic/Hardcover), 1989

Why Am I Different? by Norma Simon (Albert Whitman & Co.), 1993

Your Dad Was Just Like You by Dolores Johnson (Simon & Schuster), 1993

EXPLAINING WHAT YOU WANT
ASSERTIVENESS

To see what is right and not to do it, is want of courage.

–Confucius

With a good base of such communication skills such as empathy and self-management having been developed from activities in the previous chapter, students will be able to progress into the next stage of relationship building–handling someone else's emotions. When students are able to empathize with others and manage their own emotions, they can then begin to develop social competencies that make for effectiveness in dealing with others. You might say that their "people skills" are ready to ripen! Without being able to handle conflicts and ask for what they want assertively, students will be inept in the social world.

Once these communication skills are developed, students will be able to effectively shape a social encounter, to motivate and inspire others, to thrive in intimate relationships and to put others at ease. While there are many ways to conceive of social competence, one of the more succinct is in terms of collaboration, expressiveness, self-presentation and self-preservation.

Let's face it, we are always sending signals, and those messages, explicit or implicit, affect those we are with. Well-developed communication or social skills allow us to effectively manage an emotional exchange. *Popular* and *charming* are terms we use for people we like to be with because their emotional qualities and communication skills make us feel good. People who are able to resolve a conflict, help others soothe their feelings and explain exactly how they feel and what they want, have especially valued social commodities. These are the individuals to whom others turn in greatest emotional need. Whether we like it or not, we are all part of one another's tool kit for social and emotional change. Hopefully for better, rather than worse.

EXPLAINING WHAT YOU WANT
THEME OBJECTIVES

1. COLLABORATE WHEN RESOLVING CONFLICTS

Conflict in any group, classroom or situation at school is usually counterproductive. When conflict is present, cooperative groups stop functioning, productivity diminishes and emotions cloud reason. Have you ever noticed that you really can't power your way through a student conflict? Using your power as teacher may get the warring factions to stop momentarily, but eventually you must use the art of collaborative communication to resolve the problem. If you want to motivate your students, you don't have the luxury of ignoring conflict. You must let students know that you expect them to participate in resolving conflicts. If you are to build a strong classroom community, students must be able to disagree in a healthy manner, but to live in harmony they cannot function under the threat of an unresolved conflict.

2. DEVELOP ASSERTION SKILLS

It is important to teach our students how to clearly and tactfully communicate to others what they need and expect. Doing so will help them to get what they want. Students must become good at communicating their needs and letting others know how they feel. It's ridiculous to expect others to figure out how we feel through brain waves or hidden messages.

3. HANDLE HURTFUL MESSAGES

It's inevitable—children are going to get in fights, arguments and name-calling battles. When they do, it becomes imperative that they have a way to protect themselves emotionally. Handling hurtful messages is a skill that can be developed. Acquiring skills by which to turn hurtful messages into harmless messages helps students to be responsible for their own feelings. It isn't the event that affects how they feel, but rather what they think of the event that makes the difference. Students can learn to make choices about the way they feel.

SHAPE UP

GOAL: Students will collaborate in cooperative teams to create specific shapes.

TIME: 20 minutes

SETTING: classroom

PROCEDURE:

If your students wish to be successful conflict resolution managers, then they must learn how to collaborate. Collaboration pulls people together, instead of pulling people apart. And every class should strive to be a cohesive whole, not a chaotic bunch of squabblers. This activity should help your students shape up into a cooperative, collaborating class.

The first step is to get students up and out of their seats. This activity has many variations, so choose one that suits your needs. Ask students to form a shape. Your class can form geometric shapes: triangles, squares, circles, etc.; geographic shapes: countries, states, continents or just about any shape. You may ask them, for example, to shape up into the word *team*. As soon as they have mastered this, ask them to transform themselves into a second shape, such as the word *work*.

Once your students are back in their seats, ask them to reflect on the activity. How did they work as a team? Did anyone assume a leadership role? Did anyone help the team by offering to move to a different place? How did it feel when they successfully created the shape together? How could they improve next time?

You can use this activity as an opener to a lesson, as an assessment for understanding concepts of new vocabulary words or just to get your class active and moving. The next time you do this lesson, challenge your students to create a different shape without talking. Your students are sure to shape up into cooperative collaborators!

NASTY OR NICE?

GOAL: Students will rephrase personal statements into behavioral statements to create a more positive effect.

TIME: 30 minutes

SETTING: classroom

MATERIALS: worksheet on page 101, pencil

PROCEDURE:

All teachers spend time moderating student conflicts which reduces precious instructional time. When a student is accused of acting or "being" nasty, he or she will usually become defensive. This activity will help your students rephrase their nasty accusations into comments that can lead to a positive change.

First, ask your students if anyone likes to be judged, condemned or blamed. No? No kidding! Not too many people do! Your students should agree that nobody wants to be told that they are a nasty or mean person. However, there are occasions when people do nasty or mean things. So, when your students deal with a negative situation, they need to address the person's behavior, not the person. This means that they should avoid making comments about what they think the person is, such as, "Maria is a tattletale." Maria is likely to immediately respond, "I am not!" What they should focus on is making a statement about what the person does that they would like to change, such as, "Maria tells the teacher about everything she sees." This statement can now be evaluated more objectively. Either Maria does or does not tell the teacher about everything she sees.

Once students have differentiated between commenting on who they think a person is, as opposed to what they think a person does, have them rephrase the comments on the "Nasty or Nice?" worksheet. Each statement is a somewhat nasty way of commenting on a person's personality. See if your students find a nicer way to comment on what the person is *doing*.

Here are some possible answers to the "Nasty or Nice?" worksheet:
1. "Luis, you've talked while I was talking twice."
2. "Lisa talks loudly."
3. "Clara works slowly on her math."
4. "Juan ate with his mouth open."
5. "Serita, you seem to think of only one solution."
6. "Chris, it bothers me when you keep poking me."
7. "Carrie, you look unhappy about your test grade."
8. "Cory, you did not touch third base."

TLC10081 Copyright © Teaching & Learning Company, Carthage, IL 62321-0010

Name _____

Nasty or Nice?

If you'd like a classmate to change behavior, you'll probably have more success if you follow these rules. First, don't make a comment about what you think he or she *is*. Second, do talk about what he or she *does*. See if you can change these "nasty" personal comments into "nice" statements about the person's behavior. Look at the first sentence for an example.

1. "Luis, you are being rude!"

   "Luis, you've talked while I was talking twice. " _____

2. "Lisa, you're a big mouth!"

   _____

3. "Clara, you always are slow."

   _____

4. "Juan, you're a pig!"

   _____

5. "Serita, you are so stubborn!"

   _____

6. "Chris, you're being a pain!"

   _____

7. "Carrie, you're just jealous!"

   _____

8. "Cory, you never play fair!"

   _____

ARE YOU ASSERTIVE?

GOAL: This activity will help students to discern between three different communication modes. They will learn that the most effective mode is assertive.

TIME: 45 minutes

SETTING: classroom

MATERIALS: tape recorder, blank cassette, worksheets on pages 104 and 105 and pencils

PROCEDURE:

Before this activity can be done in class, use the **bold** quotations on page 104 in order to make a tape recording of different voices reacting to various scenarios. The more voices you can record, the more fun your students will have with this activity. You can introduce the people recorded on your tape as real people that you have encountered recently.

When your recording is finished and queued to the beginning, you are ready to start the activity by illustrating the difference between three different communication modes.

Make three columns on the chalkboard with the headings *Aggressive*, *Assertive* and *Passive*. Then write words that define the terms underneath these headings. The example to follow has 1) personality descriptions, 2) metaphors and 3) quotations to illustrate the three communication modes.

Say to your students, "When we talk to others, the best way to communicate what we want and need is by doing so assertively. When we're aggressive, we tend to hurt feelings or anger those who we talk to. There is no need to use force when communicating what we want and need."

AGGRESSIVE	**ASSERTIVE**	**PASSIVE**
1. Bully, pushy; uses too much force to get what he/she wants or needs.	Gets what he/she wants with just the right amount of power	Wishy-washy, weak, whiny. Often this person acts like he/she has no power to get what he/she wants or needs.
2. Bulldozer	Computer	Leaky faucet
3. "Move over, you jerk!"	"Will you please move over; I don't have enough room."	"You are always crowding me; I never have any space."

❝ On the other hand, when we talk passively, we don't come across as strong communicators. Often when we are passive, people ignore us. Our wants and needs don't get communicated clearly and we end up not getting what we want and need."

The best way to communicate is to do so assertively. Being assertive simply means that you clearly state what you want and need. There is no confusion about what the speaker wants and needs when he or she is assertive. When a person acts assertively, they send a clear message to the listener that they expect some response to take place."

Next, go over the description on the board until you are satisfied that your students have a basic understanding of the three communication methods.

Here is where the tape recordings come in! Tell your students that you will play a recording of some different voices. Pretend that you captured the voices during real situations.

Say to your students, "I would like you to simply put an X in the appropriate column after listening to the speaker. For example, after hearing the first speaker, decide whether the person sounded Aggressive, Assertive or Passive. Make your decision by putting an X in just one of the columns for speaker 1. I will help you to keep track of who is talking by putting the number of the speaker on the board. We will be listening to 10 voices altogether.

VOICES: AGGRESSIVE, PASSIVE OR ASSERTIVE?

Say, "The first voice you hear is someone responding to buying an apple at the store that had a worm in it." Play the tape.

1. "I am going to bring this apple back and stick it in the grocer's face!"

Stop the recording now and let your students mark the appropriate column.
Resume. "The second voice you hear is someone asking for extra ketchup at a restaurant.

2. "I wish I had some ketchup for these French fries."

Continue introducing the quotations. "The third voice is of someone asking another to make room for him on the bus."

3. "I need a little more room; could you move over, please?"

"The next voice is of someone who wants attention from her mother."

4. "You never listen to anything I say."

"The fifth voice is of someone who has waited a long time in line for theater tickets."

5. "This line is the slowest line in the world. Are all the workers sleeping?"

"The next voice is of a teacher who needs her students' attention."

6. "I will wait for everyone to get quiet before I continue speaking."

"The seventh voice is of a student who has been waiting a long time to be called on."

7. "That's it, since you won't call on me, I will scream out my answer!"

"The next voice is of a mother talking to her son."

8. "If you don't come here right now, I'll smack you!"

"Speaker number nine is a boy who wants to play with his friend's toy truck."

9. "Hey, Rodney, can I play with that?"

"The last speaker is a girl talking to the student sitting next to her."

10. "The teacher hasn't picked me as a monitor this whole year."

After students have responded to each voice, discuss their answers. It may be necessary to play the tape a second time. Then give the students the answers so they can assess their learning.

Answers:

1. Aggressive	5. Can be considered either Passive or Aggressive	7. Aggressive
2. Passive		8. Aggressive
3. Assertive		9. Assertive
4. Passive	6. Assertive	10. Passive

104

Name _____

HOW ARE THESE COMMUNICATORS?

Directions: Listen to the voices on the tape recorder and decide which communication mode each person is using. Is the speaker aggressive, assertive or passive? Indicate your decision by putting an *X* in just one of the columns for each voice.

	AGGRESSIVE	ASSERTIVE	PASSIVE
1.	_____	_____	_____
2.	_____	_____	_____
3.	_____	_____	_____
4.	_____	_____	_____
5.	_____	_____	_____
6.	_____	_____	_____
7.	_____	_____	_____
8.	_____	_____	_____
9.	_____	_____	_____
10.	_____	_____	_____

How well do you understand communication styles?

To find out, match your scores with these descriptions:

9-10 Correct = Very well!

7-8 Correct = Pretty well

5-6 = Sort of

0-4 = Try again!

I'M RATIONAL!

GOAL: Students will learn how to develop rational "I" statements in order to avoid conflict when attempting to solve a problem.

TIME: 30 minutes

SETTING: classroom

MATERIALS: worksheet on page 107, pencil

PROCEDURE:

Here's a great activity for helping students develop the skills for dealing with a conflict. Effective communicators want to have their message heard and acted upon by the listener. They want to reduce resistance. Resistance is created when the listener feels blamed or attacked. When the listener's defenses go up, their ability to cooperate and change their behavior goes down.

An easy way to reduce resistance is to communicate with I-Rational statements instead of You-Blaming statements. The key to a successful I-Rational approach is for the speaker to say the message in a nonblaming manner and take responsibility for his or her feelings. This is done by objectively stating the behavior that is causing conflict followed by an "I" statement explaining the speaker's feelings. For example, the speaker states the listener's behavior, "When you ignore me . . . " then states his or her feelings, "I feel mad because I need help with my homework so I can get all A's this quarter." This statement should begin the process towards making a change in the listener's behavior.

Listen to the difference when the same statement is made using the You-Blaming approach. "You make me mad! You never pay any attention to me! I'll never get all A's this quarter because you never help me with my homework!" You can imagine the amount of resistance building in the listener. Instead of working towards a solution, the listener would feel a need to defend himself. Obviously the I-Rational approach is a more effective means of resolving conflict!

After you have contrasted the I-Rational and You-Blaming approaches with students, have them work out a problem using the "I'm Rational!" worksheet. First have your students record a problem regarding another person's behavior in a nonblaming manner in the first column. In the second column, your students write an "I"-statement about their feelings. The third column is for the consequences of the behavior for the student. Finally, your students should make an I-Rational statement using the sentence fragments at the bottom of the page. For homework, they can test their I-Rational statement to see how effectively they can communicate and resolve conflicts!

TLC10081 Copyright © Teaching & Learning Company, Carthage, IL 62321-0010

Name _____

I'm Rational!

Have you ever had a problem with a friend? How about with your family? You may not have been sure how to communicate the problem effectively and arrive at an agreeable solution. This activity will help you develop your conflict resolution skills. First, listen to your teacher's explanation of an I-Rational approach to stating problems. Then fill out the chart below. By the bottom of the page, you should have an effective way of solving your problem!

Objective Statement About the Problematic Behavior	My Feelings	Consequences for Me

Now summarize the information above with an I-Rational statement.

When you _____
(behavior)

I feel _____
(feelings)

because _____
(consequences)

INSULT TRANSFORMER

GOAL: Students will develop the ability to turn hurtful messages into something positive.

TIME: 50 minutes

SETTING: classroom

MATERIALS: variety of art supplies including but not limited to clay, shoe boxes, construction paper, shopping bags, markers, glue, cardboard boxes, paint, craft sticks and copies of the "INsults" and "Transformed OUTsults" worksheets

PROCEDURE:

We all choose to interpret or frame different events and circumstances as we wish. We can interpret things negatively or positively. We can listen to someone insult us or hurt us and then introject the insult without any editing or giving any thought as to the problems of the sender or the larger picture. Or we can all use our power to transform what we hear so that what goes on in our minds is positive rather than negative.

Have you ever noticed how students seem to swallow whole the small little insults that they receive from careless others? If someone tells them something, it seems to automatically become true. Or it automatically hurts. Here is a little activity that will help your students to take those insults or hurtful words and do something with them other than introject them. It's called the Insult Transformer–a sort of make-believe machine that changes any insult into something much less harmful.

Tell your students that they will design a transformer machine that has the power to change bad news, mean words, insults or unkind acts into something good. Explain that the only design stipulations are that their transformer machines should have three parts: an opening where words go in, an exit where the transformed information can come out and a compartment where the transforming magic occurs. Students can work in cooperative, communicative groups when building their transformer machines. They can use cardboard boxes or whatever is available. Inspire a little creativity here!

Once the transformer machines have been constructed, pass out one "INsults" worksheet to each group. Have students write their often heard and hurtful insults on the lines provided. Discuss the insults that they have generated in a very serious way. Ask about how they have felt in the past when they were the recipients of these insults. Ask them if they have ever said such insulting things themselves. Talk with them about the seriousness of these hurtful messages. Then ask them if they would like to stop these insults and change them into something better. Hopefully by now they'll be willing to promote a little compassion in your classroom.

If they all agree that it would be a good idea to change this insult tendency, then pass out one "Transformed OUTsults" worksheet to each group. Ask the groups to rewrite each insult into a transformed version. For example: "You are so stupid" can become "I wish I could be as funny as you are." The interesting aspect of this exercise is that insults will be transformed differently for each group. Once your class has completed the "Transformed OUTsults" worksheets, compare the results.

Yes, the Insult Transformer machine is a gimic to get your students thinking about changing negatives into positives, but just watch how enthusiastically they transform those insults!

Name _____

INsults

Everybody has been insulted at least once in their life. And probably almost everybody has insulted another. Insults aren't a good thing, but unfortunately they seem to be a part of living. What kind of insults have you heard? What kind of insults do you use? With your group, write the most common insults that you have heard or used. Make sure you don't actually tell an insult to someone in your group, just bring those insults to mind. Get them out in the open.

1. _____

2. _____

3. _____

4. _____

5. _____

6. _____

7. _____

8. _____

9. _____

10. _____

11. _____

12. _____

TRANSFORMED **OUT**SULTS

Now that you have all your commonly heard or used insults listed, it is time to use your brains or Insult Transformer machine to actually change those insults into something a little more positive. Call it a sort of defense against insults. With your group, take time to transform those insults into something a little more positive. So the next time you hear an insult such as those listed, instead of getting hurt, you'll be able to come OUT with something better!

1. _____

2. _____

3. _____

4. _____

5. _____

6. _____

7. _____

8. _____

9. _____

10. _____

11. _____

12. _____

To Mend a Broken Heart

GOAL: Students will create a series of personal affirmations that they can always call on when bad things happen to them.

TIME: 50 minutes

SETTING: classroom

MATERIALS: "Broken Heart" worksheet per student, "Bandages" worksheet per student, glue, pencils, construction paper, lined paper, one clothespin per student and various colored markers

PROCEDURE:

As much as we try to avoid it, everybody gets their feelings hurt once in a while. It's a part of life! Sometimes when things are going rough, we get our feelings hurt so much that it seems as though our heart has been broken. This two-part activity will help to mend your broken-hearted students. You can complete both parts on the same day or space them out over two days. For the first part, give each student a marker, a piece of construction paper and one clothespin. Students can help each other pin the piece of construction paper to their backs.

Invite students to walk around the room and write compliments or positive words about the person whose paper they write on. Students should try to write on as many persons' backs as possible. Give students approximately 15 minutes to complete this part of the activity.

After your students have written on most everyone's backs, ask them to return to their seats and to write as many positive things about themselves on a blank piece of lined paper as they can. Instruct them not to take the construction paper off their backs until you tell them to. Students with a lot of confidence should have no problem writing positively about themselves. Those lacking in self-awareness and confidence may have a more difficult time. Once your students have exhausted all the positive words that they can think of to write about themselves, allow them to take the "hidden" pieces of construction paper off their backs.

Now, hand out the "Broken Heart" and "Bandages" worksheets. Instruct students to write their five favorite statements on the bandages. They will glue their bandages onto their broken hearts. You may laminate these hearts and allow students to keep them in their desks for use whenever they need a pick-me-up.

BROKEN HEART

Everybody gets their feelings hurt once in a while. It seems to be a fact of life. We all try to act like "tough guys" now and then saying something like, "Nothing bothers me!" But everyone knows what it feels like to have a broken heart. So, give up the tough guy routine and admit it—you've had a broken heart at least once in your life—haven't you?

Now's the time to participate in an activity that will help everyone to get over those "broken heart" times in our lives. Use the "Bandages" worksheet to mend your broken heart.

Name _____

BANDAGES

What better than a bandage to mend your broken heart? Use the bandages to write your positive statements on. After you've written on all the bandages you'll need, make sure you put them on your broken heart.

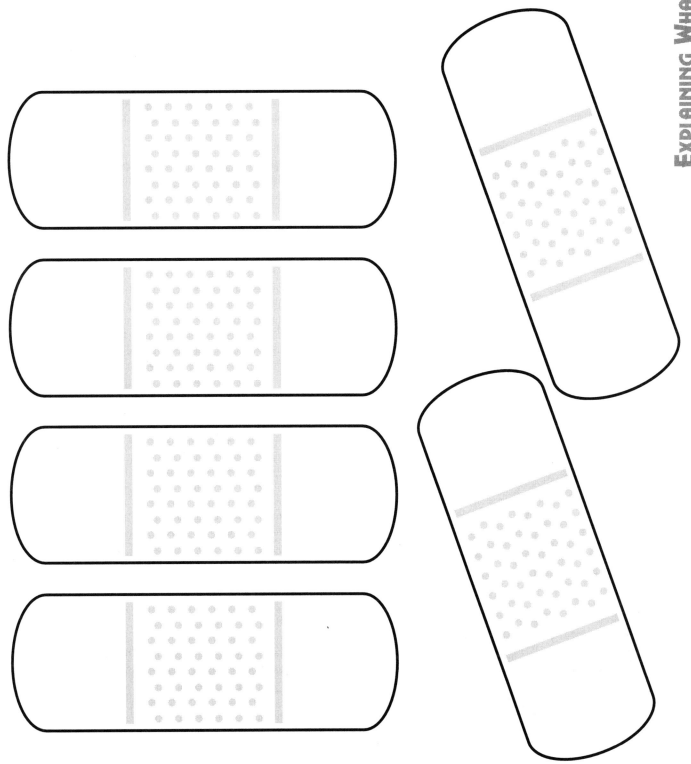

CONFLICT RESOLUTION BOX

GOAL: Students will resolve conflict through discussion.

TIME: 15-20 minutes per week

SETTING: classroom

MATERIALS: shoe box, X-acto knife or scissors, paper, pencils, "Conflict Report" worksheet, "Conflict Resolution Worksheet"

PROCEDURE:

Conflicts are inevitable among children (and adults, too!). Unfortunately for teachers, they often happen in the middle of a stellar lesson or just after recess when you were hoping to ease into the afternoon. The cries of, "He hit me!" "Did not!" "She pushed me!" can send us over the edge. Simultaneously we're silently crying, "Why can't they just get along?" or "I don't have time for this!" With accusations flying, truth is obscured and justice lost. Over time, those conflicts that are not resolved tend to create more conflict. This vicious cycle is harmful to both your students and your sanity. So here's a relatively painless solution that starts with an old shoe box!

Cut a 1" x 6" (2.5 x 15 cm) slit in the lid of the shoe box. Next, either write *Conflict Resolution Box* on the top or the side of the box. Run off several copies of the "Conflict Report" worksheet. Cut the Conflict Reports on the cut lines. Then set the box and reports in a prominent place in your classroom. Now you're ready for a class discussion about conflict resolution that should reduce the number of accusations you hear.

Open the class discussion by asking about situations in the class that cause conflict. Focus on generalities and not specific people. Your students may mention stealing pencils, pushing in line, calling each other names, etc. Ask students to list some of the results of these conflicts when they are not resolved or discussed. They can probably come up with a lengthy list–broken friendships, hurt feelings, people getting physically hurt. Now share with your class your frustration of not having the time to adequately listen to and deal with their problems. You, however, think it is important to resolve these issues so you have made a Conflict Resolution Box to help you and to enable the children to help themselves.

Here's how the Conflict Resolution Box is used: When a student has a conflict with another person in the room, he or she fills out a Conflict Report and places it in the Conflict Resolution Box. No one needs to ask or tell you about the conflict. (You may want to establish an emergency clause for grave situations. Your whole class can decide on what constitutes an emergency.) At a designated time each week (such as recess on Friday), you will look through the Conflict Resolution Box and ask the people who are having conflicts to stay in to discuss the conflict.

Before the discussion, you may want to have the students fill out the "Conflict Resolution Worksheet." This will help the students clarify their thoughts and feelings. If you do not feel that it is necessary, then use the worksheet as a guide for facilitating the discussion. During the discussion, the students should sit facing each other. Only one student is allowed to talk at a time. Choose one student to tell her side of the story to the other student (not to you). The other student is not allowed to make any comments about the first student's version. Ask questions when clarification is needed, but continually remind the students that they are talking to each other, not to you. When the first student has finished, the second student tells his story. This time, the first student is not allowed to speak until the second student is finished. Once both students have spoken, try to come to a consensus about the facts of the conflict. For example, establish who said what, who pushed who in what order, etc. Then ask the students to decide what rules were broken and what caused them to be broken. This helps students understand each other's behavior. Now ask the students to describe how they felt during and after the conflict. Recognizing each other's feelings creates empathy. Finally, ask the students to describe to each other how they would like the conflict resolved. Perhaps apologies are necessary. Compliment the students on their ability to resolve the conflict through discussion. Hopefully, after talking to each other several times with your facilitation, your students will be able to resolve conflict by themselves.

By using a Conflict Resolution Box in your room, several goals are accomplished. Your students will feel that there is always an "ear" that is willing to hear their problems. In many situations, once students feel that they have been heard, they feel the conflict is resolved. For more serious conflicts, the conflict truly can be worked out–creating a more harmonious classroom. Finally, this method can reduce the pressure on you both by modeling conflict resolution skills that your students will eventually use on their own and by organizing time to effectively deal with the conflicts.

Note: When looking through the Conflict Resolution Box, it is not necessary to address every report. By Friday (or your designated time), some of the conflicts will be irrelevant and petty–in which case you've satisfied your students' need to be heard. By selecting the most serious conflicts or by spotting the students that seem to have repeated conflicts with each other, you can maximize your time and deal only with the conflicts that are recurring.

Conflict Report

Name: _____ Date: _____

Conflict: _____

_____

Conflict Report

Name: _____ Date: _____

Conflict: _____

_____

Conflict Report

Name: _____ Date: _____

Conflict: _____

_____

Conflict Report

Name: _____ Date: _____

Conflict: _____

_____

Conflict Report

Name: _____ Date: _____

Conflict: _____

_____

Name _____

CONFLICT RESOLUTION WORKSHEET

Describe the events that happened in order during the conflict.

1. _____

2. _____

3. _____

4. _____

5. _____

6. _____

7. _____

8. _____

9. _____

10. _____

What school or class rules were broken? _____

_____

_____

How did you feel during the conflict? How did you feel after the conflict? _____

_____

_____

_____

How should this conflict be resolved? _____

_____

_____

What could you do next time to avoid or change this conflict? _____

_____

_____

CONFLICT RESOLVERS!

GOAL: Students will resolve conflict peacefully.

SETTING: classroom, bulletin board

MATERIALS: two different colored Post-its™, pencils

PROCEDURE:

Sometimes students get stumped when they have a conflict. Their emotions may inhibit them from seeing a solution to the conflict. Here's a way to let students work out conflict among themselves while helping each other find peaceful solutions.

Designate or have your class elect several Conflict Resolvers. A Conflict Resolver should be fair and good at working out problems. They are going to be in charge of monitoring a conflict-free environment. Next, establish a bulletin board in your room as the "Place of Peace." Label the top of the board *Conflicts*. Leave enough room for a row of Post-its™. Then label the bottom row *Solutions,* again leaving enough room for a row of Post-its™.

Now invite students to write and post any conflicts they have as they occur on one of the colored Post-its™. The Conflict Resolvers will be on the look out for posted conflicts. When they see one posted, they can convene and post their solutions directly underneath the conflict. Classmates who also have ideas for solutions can advise the Conflict Resolvers. Students may be relieved at how easily their conflict turns into a peaceful solution.

LITERATURE IN SUPPORT OF EXPLAINING WHAT YOU WANT

Aunt Belle's Beach by Marjory Wunsch (Lothrop), 1994

The Berenstain Bears and the New Girl in Town by Stan Berenstain (Random), 1993

Blowing Bubbles with the Enemy by Alison Jackson (Dutton), 1993

Chester's Way by Kevin Henkes (Greenwillow), 1988

The Duck and the Owl by Hanna Johansen (Dutton), 1991

Elephant and Crocodile by Max Velthuijs (Farrar, Straus & Giroux), 1990

The Emperor's Garden by Ferida Wolff (Morrow), 1994

Enter Magneto by Eric Weiner (Random), 1994

Fearsome's Hero by Dona Schenker (Knopf), 1994

The Fight by Betty Boegehold (Bantam), 1991

Finders Keepers by Will and Nicolas (Harcourt, Brace & Co.), 1989

Friday Night at Hodges' Cafe by Tim Egan (Houghton), 1994

The Friend by John Burningham (Candlewick Press), 1994

Going the Distance by Mary J. Miller (Viking), 1994

Hurt by Janine Amos (Raintree Steck-Vaughn), 1991

Iggie's House by Judy Blume (Simon & Schuster), 1992

Irene and the Big, Fine Nickel by Irene Smalls-Hector (Little), 1991

It's Mine by Leo Lionni (Knopf), 1986

It's Not the End of the World by Judy Blume (Dell), 1986

Katie's Trunk by Ann Turner (Simon & Schuster), 1992

Mary Guy by Kilty Binger (Lothrop), 1993

Matthew & Tilly by Rebecca C. Jones (Dutton), 1991

Mean Soup by Betsy Everitt (Harcourt, Brace & Co.), 1995

Now Everybody Really Hates Me by Jane R. Martin and Patricia Marx (HarperCollins), 1993

The One Who Came Back by Joann Mazzio (Houghton Mufflin & Co.), 1992

The Pain and the Great One by Judy Blume (Simon & Schuster), 1984

Rhino & Mouse by Todd S. Palmer (Dial), 1994

Rosebud by Ludwig Bemelmans (Knopf), 1993

Sheep Dreams by Arthur A. Levine (Dial), 1993

Sitti's Secrets by Naomi S. Nye (Simon & Schuster), 1994

Slither McCreep & His Brother, Joe by Terry C. Johnston (Harcourt, Brace & Co.), 1992

Sticks & Stones & Skeleton Bones by Jamie Gilson (Lothrop), 1991

Sven's Bridge by Anita Lobel (Greenwillow), 1992

Tac's Island by Ruth Y. Radin (Troll), 1989

The Tapestry Cats by Ann Turnbull (Little), 1992

The Terrible Fight by Sharon St. Germain (Houghton), 1990

Two Good Friends by Margo Mason (Bantam Little Rooster), 1990

Whompers & Whammies: The Great Circus War by Peter Stern (Lothrop), 1994

Wilson Sat Alone by Debra Hess (Simon & Schuster), 1994

The Wimp by Kathy Caple (Houghton), 1994

The Wind and the Sun by Bernadette Watts (North-South), 1992

SPREADING PEACE

For every minute you remain angry, you give up sixty seconds of peace of mind.

–Author Unknown

Now that your students are beginning to communicate effectively, the next thing you want to do is to start thinking about the ideal. What's the ideal? Probably a world where everyone is communicating effectively. Let's call it world peace. That's an enormous task isn't it? The best place to start is right in your own classroom.

Your classroom is the best place to engage children in the process of spreading peace. When spreading peace you create a safe and nurturing learning environment that allows children to express their concerns and to arrive at creative and spontaneous solutions. Through understanding, flexibility and negotiation, children learn to resolve problems assertively without violence.

As your students begin to spread peace in the classroom through newly acquired communication skills, it then becomes appropriate to extend these abilities to address global issues. Students can do more that just solve interpersonal disputes. If given the opportunity, they can solve institutional and global issues as well. Have you ever noticed how easy it is for a child to envision a world at peace? When you and your students are very clear about your goal to spread peace, you can eliminate the discouragement that comes from the belief that violence and war are inevitable. As your students begin to spread their newly acquired skills on innovative and peaceful approaches to resolving conflict, they will be taking steps to make their great desire for world peace a reality.

SPREADING PEACE THEME OBJECTIVES

1. BECOME PEACE PROMOTERS, RESPONSIBLE FOR SOLVING THEIR OWN PROBLEMS

Do you think your students truly understand what a police officer does? Do you think the police officers should change their name to "peace" officers? And what exactly would a peace officer do? What about your students? What would they do as a peace officer at your school? Enable your students to become responsible for solving their own problems in peaceful ways.

2. DETERMINE WHAT IT MEANS TO COMMUNICATE PEACEFULLY

What exactly is this thing we call *peace*? Does it mean taking care of just oneself? Or does it denote a sense of responsibility and commitment to others and the environment? What does any peaceful situation look, sound or feel like? Do these situations have certain elements in common, or is each one separate and different? Is worldwide peace possible? And just exactly how important is this thing we call *peace*? These are all questions that you and your students can explore and determine in your peaceful, communicative classroom.

3. APPLY THEIR NEWLY ACQUIRED COMMUNICATION SKILLS TO TAKE POSITIVE SOCIAL ACTIONS TO MAKE A PEACEFUL DIFFERENCE IN THEIR SCHOOL, NEIGHBORHOOD, CITY, STATE, COUNTRY OR WORLD

Anyone can become an effective communicator. But what about actually putting those skills to use? What about actually getting out in the world to become productive, positive change agents? Inspire your students to use their newly acquired communication skills to make a

difference. Students can promote peace alone to just one, or they can work together in cooperative groups to spread peace to many. Teach your students to communicate effectively and appropriately to promote peace throughout the world.

RECIPES OF PEACE

GOAL: Students will work together to compile a list of recipes for solutions to common problems or arguments.

TIME: Initially 30 minutes

SETTING: classroom

MATERIALS: "Recipes of Peace" worksheet, pencils

PROCEDURE:

Did you ever notice that the same types of problems between students seem to arise again and again? Without the insight or foresight to handle their problems differently, students will continue to go through the same vicious cycle. Problems, problems, problems! But with a little help from you, students can actually change course if they are given the opportunity beforehand to think about how to make peace out of an otherwise unpeaceful situation.

If you really are tired of seeing the same kinds of problems in your classroom day after day, now is the time to get real and tell your students so. Tell them that you think it's time to start creating recipes for peace. Tell them you want their help in figuring out what kind of ingredients go into the making of a peaceful situation. Tell them once these recipes of peace are determined, they will help us to solve problems in the future. The recipes will help us because we can always go back and add the specific peaceful ingredients when the same silly situation arises. The recipes will actually become a way of preventing a problem rather than managing a problem.

To start this activity you'll want to model the writing of a recipe of peace to show your students how it is done. So pick a common problem that you see happening in your classroom. Then use the worksheet provided to determine what you and your students think should go into the recipe of peace for that specific problem. After you and your class have gone through this first experience of formulating a recipe of peace, your students can think of other problems that arise in class that are also in need of a recipe of peace.

Each problem may have many different recipes. The trick is to have your students determine what silly problems usually arise in class so that they can be cognitively aware of the problem at least on some level and therefore maybe avoid the problem in the future. Once you and your students have determined enough recipes of peace for all the common problems, you can put them into a decorative book with a "problem table of contents." Or if you're feeling creative, you might want to write the recipes on index cards designed by the students.

Name _____

RECIPES OF PEACE

Have you ever had a problem with one of your classmates? Would you like to turn this problem into a peaceful situation? Well, now is the time to give it a try. This activity gives you an opportunity to think of a solution or a recipe of peace for any and all problems you can think of. You may not think so right now, but there is a solution to every problem! The trick is to find out exactly what kinds of ingredients go into the solution. Take the steps provided on this worksheet and make up your own recipe of peace. If you follow these steps every time you see this problem come up in class, you can bet that peace will be sure to follow.

State the problem. What happened?

_____

_____

How do people involved in this problem usually feel?

_____

_____

How do people involved in this want to feel? Do you think they naturally want to solve the problem?

_____

_____

Now, without any help from your teacher, or anyone else, list the ingredients you think will be necessary to come to a solution. You can call this your recipe of peace.

1. _____

2. _____

3. _____

4. _____

5. _____

6. _____

THE PEN IS MIGHTIER THAN THE SWORD

GOAL: Students will become aware of the need and effectiveness of speaking out for the cause of peace.

TIME: 45 minutes

SETTING: classroom

MATERIALS: copied form letters, pens

PROCEDURE:

Often, children don't have a sense of just how much power their voices contain. But the truth is that politicians, educators and celebrities respond to children with ease and interest. Help your students to take advantage of this fact by beginning a letter writing campaign, as a preliminary step to getting involved in the peace process.

In this activity your students will first write a letter of inquiry to a national peace organization or advocate. The second part of this activity will involve your students in what could be a year-long letter writing campaign to countries and governments in need of peace advocates.

Say, "I want to introduce you to a power of yours that you may not be aware of. No, it's not the ability to fly or extrasensory perception or anything like that. The power that I'm thinking of is influence. Kids have a special voice that a lot of powerful people take very seriously. Why? Because you represent the world's future! We will be using this power to get involved in making peaceful changes in the world. But first, let's brainstorm on why peace is important to us."

Put the words *Why peace?* in a bubble and begin to web reasons to the bubble. To inspire your students to think about peace, you can start the web with a few reasons already attached. For example: So that we can spend our time doing better things than just surviving. Because arms are for hugging not for fighting.

Pass the form letter out to everyone and discuss the vocabulary and questions before passing out ballpoint pens.

Say, "An advocate is someone who speaks out for people that may not be able to speak for themselves, like babies, the elderly or people in jail. People who don't live in peaceful places need advocates to tell others about their problems so these problems aren't ignored." Write the word *advocate* on the board and alongside it the definition: "a person who speaks out for those who need help." Explain to your students that we may get the opportunity to help people locally, right here in our neighborhood or somewhere else around the world, globally. Write the word *globally* with its definition: "things happening around the world" and *locally*: "things happening close to home on the board as well."

Then go over the questions one by one in order to help students to write an informed letter. They should now be able to list a few reasons why peace is important to them. The second question in the form letter may need some prompting from you. Say, "What sorts of peace problems do you face at school or at home? Write about whichever problems you are comfortable talking about."

Using this form letter may not be for all your students. Some will be able to create an original letter by themselves. But for your students who need it, instruct them to read it and then provide the missing information. They can practice their answers on scratch paper first. Letters should be written in pen. Tell students that all business transactions including letters are done in pen.

After students have finished writing, they may share their letters with their classmates.

You are ready to determine the next step in peace advocacy for your students. Good job!

SPREADING PEACE

School Name _____
School Address _____
City, State and Zip Code _____

Dear Peace Advocate:

I am writing from _____ school where I am presently in the ____th grade.

I would like to find ways that I and my fellow students can help in furthering the cause of peace, both locally and globally.

Here are a few reasons why I feel peace is so important:

_____

_____

_____

Some of the peace problems that my school and neighborhood have are: _____

_____

_____

_____

Here are some of the areas in which I may be helpful: _____

_____

_____

_____

Please write back as soon as possible. I am anxious to get started.

Sincerely yours in peace,

_____
(your name)

126

PATH TO PEACE

GOAL: To create an ongoing sense of the importance and effectiveness of peace in the classroom.

TIME: initially 30 minutes

SETTING: classroom

MATERIALS: "Path to Peace" worksheets, pencils, markers or crayons

PROCEDURE:

Everybody's heard of the Nobel Peace Prize, right? Have your students? If not, you may want to begin this activity with a discussion on the Nobel Peace Prize. This prize, which is awarded yearly, is given to the person or persons who do more for the cause of peace than anyone else in the world. Visit your library and research the prize. Who were the past recipients of the prize? For what actions were they awarded the prize?

Once you have researched the Nobel Peace Prize to your satisfaction, explain to your students that peace is a state that is especially valuable for a nurturing learning environment. Peace is something that has to be worked on. It doesn't always come easily.

Then say, "Just to show everyone, including visitors to the class, how important peace is to this classroom, we are going to form a "path to peace" that will start in this classroom and can (with a little imagination) actually be taken out into the yard, into the cafeteria and to who knows where?"

Now for the challenge! Ask your class, "If there were a Peace Prize at this school, what could you do to win it? How could you further the cause of peace for our school?" Brainstorm ideas. Next have the students choose ideas which they can actually implement. Once they have chosen ideas, ask them to illustrate and explain what they could do so that the whole class can eventually have a "path to peace" on the classroom wall. Let children know that they can add to the path at anytime. Construct your "path to peace" on your wall and let it wind around the entire room.

When unpeaceful situations come up in class, have students think about what piece of their path is missing that would have helped to solve the problem.

PATH TO PEACE

PATH TO PEACE

An Officer and a Gentleperson

Goal: To familiarize students with the duties and challenges of a police officer (also known here as peace officer); to clarify how peace officers and students can be helpful to one another.

Time: 60 minutes

Setting: the classroom or a police station

Materials: "My Interview with a Peace Officer" worksheet

Procedure:

Many communities have adversarial relationships with their police departments. This is extremely defeating as most of the men and women serving their communities as police officers do an excellent and oftentimes heroic job. This activity seeks to create an intimate and safe setting in which students may interview an officer as well as to confront some of the misconceptions that they may hold about those working in law enforcement.

The activity requires some planning time, however, most police departments have officers who are devoted to public outreach. Arranging a classroom visit should be a fairly simple task.

First, schedule an in-class visit or a field trip to your local police station. Second, prepare students ahead of time by letting them know of your intended visitor. Tell your students that the visit is expressly for their questions. Then organize your class into groups of four to six students. On the day that the officer arrives, each student will be allowed to ask one question, therefore groups of students should come up with four to six individual questions with each student taking ownership of one. As a result, all students will have at least four to six questions to which they will be seeking answers.

DEVELOPING INTERVIEW QUESTIONS

STEP 1

Encourage students to come up with their own questions by writing a few questions on the board to get them thinking. The following question suggestions touch on various elements of a police or "peace" officer's job. Write a few on the board that seem most relevant to your community.

- How do you get along with the people you serve?

- What can we do to prevent crime from affecting us?

- If you could change anything about your job, what would it be?

- Should we be afraid of you?

- How do police officers help kids?

- How can we get in touch with you if we need you?

STEP 2

Then say, "On scratch paper I would like you to write at least one good question that you will ask our visitor from the _____ Police Department. You may get ideas from the questions that I have written on the board, however, I would like you to come up with your own question–something that you're really curious about, angry about or uncertain of. After you have thought of your question, I'd like you to share yours with your group.

STEP 3

Begin this third step by saying, "I will now pass out an interview form. Before writing your question on this sheet, go through the checklist at the top of the sheet to make sure that your question is a good interview question. If you can answer *yes* to the questions at the top of your interview sheet, then you may write your question on the first line. If you answer *no* to any of the three questions on the top of your interview sheet, try to change your question so that you will be able to answer *yes* to all three questions."

"Next, if your group mates can answer *yes* to the questions at the top about their questions, then you may write the questions of all your group mates on the following lines of your interview sheet. When you are finished, your interview sheet should have your question on it as well as the questions of all the people in your group." On the day of the visit, students will have four to six prepared questions written on their interview sheets. They will be seeking answers to their own question and writing the answers of their group mates' questions on their interview form. Tell students that as interviewers seeking information, they will often have the necessity to say, "Can you please repeat what you just said?" in order to write the answers on their sheets.

Option: After the interview, students can compile their answers for a question and answer sheet to share with the rest of the school as a peace outreach activity.

Name _____   Date _____

MY INTERVIEW WITH A PEACE OFFICER

*If you can answer **yes** to these three questions, you
are ready to write your questions on this sheet.*

- Does your question require an answer
with more words than just *yes* or *no*?
- Do you and your group mates understand your question?
- Are you truly interested in what the answer to your question is?

1. Question: _____

    Answer: _____

    _____

2. Question: _____

    Answer: _____

    _____

3. Question: _____

    Answer: _____

    _____

4. Question: _____

    Answer: _____

    _____

5. Question: _____

    Answer: _____

    _____

6. Question: _____

    Answer: _____

    _____

PEACE POLL

GOAL: Students will fill out a poll to expand their understanding of the word *peace*.

TIME: 30 minutes

SETTING: classroom

MATERIALS: Peace Poll forms, pencils

PROCEDURE:

Tell your students that the class is going to work to fully understand the word *peace*. In order to begin, a definition of the word needs to be developed. It is important to note that even a mature understanding of the word *peace* evolves; any definition for *peace* shouldn't be presented as if it were the only one.

Hand out and explain the Peace Poll sheet, allowing those students whose understanding of the form is clear to work through it independently. Some of your students may need you to read and explain the form, question by question. Once your students have completed the worksheet, facilitate a brief discussion on your students' responses. Ask if any of the questions were difficult to answer and try to point out the variety of responses given. After everyone is done, collect the sheets and compile the data for the next activity–graphing the results.

Name _____

PEACE POLL

What do you know about peace? What do your classmates know about peace? Read each question carefully and then write your answer on the lines provided. You may write Y for *yes* and N for *no*.

1. What is the first word or words that come into your mind when you think about *peace*?

   _____

2. Where do you think the most peaceful place in your school is? Why?

   _____

   _____

3. Is there peace in your home? Yes or No? _____ Can you explain why?

   _____

   _____

4. Is there peace in your neighborhood? Yes or No? _____ Can you explain why?

   _____

   _____

5. Do you think most of the world is peaceful? Yes or No? _____ Why?

   _____

   _____

6. Do you think people or countries have to like each other in order to have peace? Yes or No? _____ Why?

   _____

   _____

7. Name all the places that you know about in the world where there isn't peace right now.

   _____

   _____

PEACE POLL BAR GRAPH

GOAL: Students will be able to assess how their understanding of the word *peace* coincides with their classmates.

TIME: 30 minutes

SETTING: classroom

MATERIALS: one to four "Peace Poll Bar Graph" worksheet(s) for each student, tagboard, fat colored markers

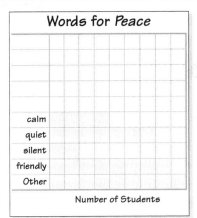

PROCEDURE:

Before you begin this activity, analyze the data compiled from the "Peace Poll" activity and prepare a bar graph on a large piece of lined tagboard reflecting students' results.

PREPARING YOUR PEACE POLL BAR GRAPHS

First you'll want to know what the results were for question one. Depending on the number of responses or words given for this question you may require one Peace Poll Bar Graph alone. Graph the results for the most popular words that enter your students' minds when thinking of the word *peace*. Add up all the other words and reflect the number of other words in an adjacent bar called *other*.

Second, graph the results of the question two the same way as the first. For example, if the most common answer to the question "Where do you think the most peaceful place in your school is?" are the library, the office and the classroom, add up the amount of students who gave these answers. Graph them individually. For all other answers to this question construct a bar called *other*.

Graphing the results of questions three to six is simple. For each of the following questions, tally up and graph all the yes and no responses. Is there peace in your home? Is there peace in your neighborhood? Do you think most of the world is peaceful? Do you think people or countries have to like each other in order to have peace?

Finally, graph the answers to question seven the same way you did questions one and two.

As soon as you have compiled the data onto a bar graph, you are ready to talk with your students about their understanding of the word *peace*. Discuss the results of each question with your students. To inspire discussion on the first question, you may write the words *accepting others for who they are* on the board. Say, "These are some of the words that I think of when I hear the word *peace*." For the second question, students will most likely write places such as the school library, the classroom and the office. Now is the time to ask students their reasons for writing these and other locations. Ask, "Why do you consider these places peaceful?"

For questions three through six, point out the number of yes and no responses to your students. Ask for comments. Can students draw any conclusions from these answers?

For the last question, be prepared to hear some off-the-wall answers! Make sure to ask for explanations. You may also write the names of some of the current warring areas in the world. Ask students if they have ever heard of these places.

Name _____

PEACE POLL BAR GRAPH

Now is the time to work with your fellow classmates to graph all the responses to each of the questions. Work with your teacher to determine how many bars you will need for each question. Make sure you label your graph properly! What do these results say about you and your classmates' understanding of the word *peace*?

Question number(s) _____

Name _____

Dove Tale

Perhaps you have seen the symbol of the dove flying with a twig of laurel. That dove is often used as a symbol of peace. When you call a person a "dove," that means they are an advocate of peace. Inside the dove below, write a short story about a person who acted as a dove in a hostile conflict. Use your new conflict resolution skills to describe how he or she avoided or reduced the hostilities during the conflict.

When you've finished, cut out your dove. Then tie a string to its head so you can display the dove in your classroom!

MONITORING THE NEWS FOR PEACE

GOAL: Students will analyze a newscast for its peace content.

TIME: 90 minutes

SETTING: classroom

MATERIALS: videocassette tape of a 30-minute local nightly news broadcast, VCR, "Peace Log" worksheet for every student

PREPARATION: Tape a 30-minute news broadcast to play for your class.

PROCEDURE:

Tell students that they will watch and analyze a news program. Also explain to them that later on tonight, you would like them to repeat the activity for homework.

Hand out one "Peace Log" worksheet to each student and explain how it is to be used. Say, "This worksheet will help us to make judgements about the stories that we will see. We will decide if the stories we view are about peace or not. In addition, we will identify the content by writing a few words of description about each story."

You will need to model this activity by playing the broadcast and stopping it after the first story. Ask your students if they think the story had anything to do with peace. If yes, put a check mark in the first box next to the word *peace*. If it is a violent story, a story about a storm, an earthquake or any other volatile situation, put a mark in the Not Peace box. Write a few words about the story on the set of lines under the appropriate word.

Go through the same procedure for a few different stories. Select a story from the weather report and the sports report to model how Peace or Not Peace is exhibited in these news areas.

Extension: Assign your students to watch a 30-minute nighttime news broadcast for homework.

Name _____

PEACE LOG

Tonight you will watch a 30-minute news program on television. For each news story, put a check (✓) next to the word that describes the story best. Is it more like Peace than Not Peace, or is the story about something that has nothing to do with the subject of peace? Then try to write a few words for each story under the word that describes the story best.

PEACE ☐ ☐ ☐ ☐ ☐

1. _____
2. _____
3. _____
4. _____
5. _____

NOT PEACE ☐ ☐ ☐ ☐ ☐

1. _____
2. _____
3. _____
4. _____
5. _____

NEITHER ☐ ☐ ☐ ☐ ☐

1. _____
2. _____
3. _____
4. _____
5. _____

CONCLUSION

Did you notice more peaceful stories or more not peaceful stories in the news broadcast that

you watched? _____

Why do you think that is? _____

_____

What kind of stories would you like to see more often? _____

Why? _____

Which news program did you watch? _____

INGREDIENTS OF PEACE

GOAL: Students will find common elements in various situations in which peace is present.

TIME: 30 minutes

SETTING: classroom

MATERIALS: "Peace Log" worksheets, "Ingredients of Peace" worksheets, pencils, two pieces of bread, peanut butter, jelly, honey, pickles, raisins, bananas

PROCEDURE:

Begin by asking students to take out their "Peace Log" homework on which they analyzed a news broadcast. Explain to them that they will soon be filling in the conclusion section of the sheet in class.

Next, with the various ingredients for a peanut butter and jelly sandwich, say to the students, "I am going to make a peanut butter and jelly sandwich." Begin to spread the peanut butter on one piece of bread and then the jelly on the other. Say, "There are different ways to make this kind of sandwich. Some people mix the peanut butter and jelly before spreading it; some people put both the jelly and the peanut butter on the same piece of bread. Some people like to put raisins on the sandwich (do this now), some people like to add bananas (do this now), some people use honey instead of jelly (hold up the honey) and some people actually put pickles in their sandwiches (hold up a jar of pickles). But the important thing to remember is that however you do it and whatever you choose to put on your sandwich, there are always three common ingredients, bread, jelly and peanut butter.

Now ask your students: "Now that you know the common ingredients for something as simple as a peanut butter and jelly sandwich, it is time to figure out what the common ingredients are of a peaceful story. So, did you notice any common ingredients in all the peace stories that you saw on television that you also listed on your Peace Log?" With your group mates, come up with as many common ingredients as you can for the peaceful situations.

Now you are ready to finish the worksheet. Where it says *conclusion,* write the cooperative group discussions, sifting out the common ingredients for peace.

Name _____

INGREDIENTS OF PEACE

What do you think is common in all the stories and situations of peace that you saw on the newscast that you watched?

- Are people angry with each other?
- Are they respectful of each other?
- Did they listen to each other?
- How was peace reached?
- Did two sides of an issue become one in the end?
- What happened?
- Was there always peace right from the beginning of the relationship or did the people involved go through a period of conflict and then settle their differences and move into peace?

List the common ingredients of peace below.

1. _____

2. _____

3. _____

4. _____

5. _____

6. _____

Now that you have discovered the common ingredients of peace, how do you think you can apply those ingredients in your interactions with others at your school?

_____

_____

_____

PEACE/POLICE

GOAL: Students will expand their definitions on the roles of a police officer.

TIME: 30 minutes

SETTING: classroom

MATERIALS: "Peace/Police" worksheet, dictionaries, pencils, paper

PROCEDURE:

Divide students into partner pairs. Pass out one "Peace/Police" worksheet and one dictionary to each pair. Ask students to find and write the dictionary definitions for both words on their sheet.

When they are finished writing, ask students to compare and contrast the meanings of the two words. For example: *Police* is an aggressive, action-oriented word; *peace* is a description of well-being. Comparing is the process of examining two or more objects, ideas or people for the purpose of identifying similarities and differences. Finding differences is usually referred to as contrasting but noting differences is still considered a skill of comparing so you want to make sure to invite your students to come up with ways that the two words are similar. Say, "Think about how both words work, and then figure out what they have in common."

The next step in this activity entails filling in a Venn diagram. When you have a sense that your students have grasped at least some similarities and some differences in the words *peace* and *police*, they are ready to fill in the Venn diagram at the bottom of their "Peace/Police" worksheets.

Explain that they will be filling in the left circle of the diagram with the things that the word *peace* has that *police* does not have. The right side of the diagram is just the opposite–fill in all the things that *police* means that are different from the meanings of *peace*. The space common to both circles is for all the things the two words have in common. Challenge students to fill in the whole diagram.

Lastly, make a master Venn diagram on the chalkboard as a generator for more discussion. Fill it with your students' responses.

Name _____

Peace/Police

Directions

1. Write the definitions for both words.
2. Wait for your teacher's instructions on what to do next.
3. Fill in the Venn diagram.

PEACE: _____   **POLICE:** _____

_____ | _____
_____ | _____
_____ | _____
_____ | _____
_____ | _____
_____ | _____
_____ | _____
_____ | _____

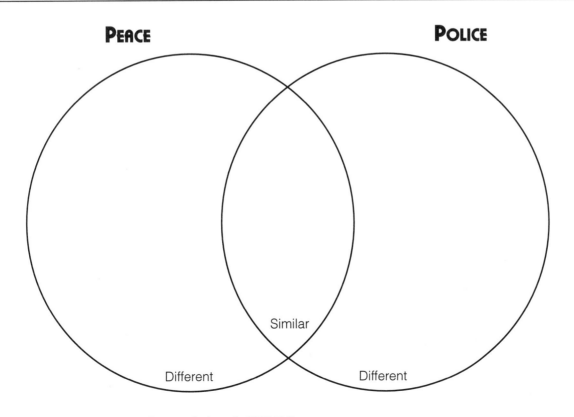

PEACE   POLICE

Similar

Different   Different

LITERATURE IN SUPPORT OF SPREADING PEACE

The Animal Family by Randall Jarrell (HarperCollins), 1995

The Big Book for Peace by Ann Durell and Marilyn Sachs (Dutton), 1990

Casey Over There by Staton Rabin (Harcourt), 1994

The Christmas Witch by Steven Kellogg (Dial), 1992

A Dragon in the Family by Jackie F. Koller (Little), 1993

The Emperor's Garden by Ferida Wolff (Tambourine), 1994

The Flame of Peace: A Tale of the Aztecs by Deborah N. Lattimore (HarperCollins), 1991

Flon Flon and Annette by Elzbieta (Holt), 1994

Forest by Janet T. Lisle (Orchard), 1993

For Every Child, a Better World by Louise Gikow and Ellen Weiss (Muppet Press), 1993

Grandfather's Dream by Holly Keller (Greenwillow), 1994

The Knight Who Was Afraid to Fight by Barbara S. Hazen (Dial), 1994

The Little Prince by Antoine de Saint-Exupery (Harcourt), 1993

The Long Search by Christine Pullein-Thompson (Simon & Schuster), 1993

Making Friends Sponsored by Children as Peacemakers Foundation (Henry Holt), 1987

Over the Deep Blue Sea by Daisaku Ikeda (Knopf), 1993

Peace Begins with You by Katherine Scholes (Little), 1994

Peace on the Playground: Nonviolent Ways of Problem Solving by Eileen Lucas (Watts), 1991

Rebel by Allan Baillie (Ticknor & Fields Books), 1994

The Return of the Indian by Lynne R. Banks (Doubleday), 1986

Ruby Mae Has Something to Say by David Small (Crown), 1992

Shades of Gray by Carolyn Reeder (Avon), 1991

Sitti's Secrets by Naomi S. Nye (Simon & Schuster), 1994

Smoky Night by Eve Bunting (Harcourt), 1994

Spinning Tales, Weaving Hope by Ed Brody (New Society), 1992

Stepping on the Cracks by Mary Downing Hahn (Avon), 1992

The Story of Ferdinand by Munro Leaf (Viking), 1936

Taking a Stand Against Nuclear War by Ellen Thro (Watts), 1990

Talking Walls by Margy B. Knight (Tilbury House), 1995

The United Nations by R. Stein (Childrens Press), 1994

The War with Grandpa by Robert K. Smith (Dell), 1995

What Did You Lose, Santa? by Berthe Amoss (Harper), 1987

Who Belongs Here? An American Story by Margy B. Knight and Anne S. O'Brien (Tilbury House), 1993

Wildflower Tea by Ethel Pochocki (Simon & Schuster), 1993

Women of Peace: Nobel Peace Prize Winners by Anne Schraff (Enslow), 1994

You Can Go Home Again by Jirina Marton (Firefly Books Ltd.), 1994

144